Anchored In Truth Exploring The Depths of Psalm 119

Joshua Rhoades

Published by Joshua Paul Rhoades, 2024.

ANCHORED IN TRUTH EXPLORING THE DEPTHS OF PSALM 119

First edition. September 1, 2024.

ISBN: 979-8224976621

Written by Joshua Rhoades.

Also by Joshua Rhoades

Courage Under Fire: David's Stand On The Battlefield

Jonah's Journey: Voices Of Redemption And Lessons In Obedience

The Furnace Of Faith: 12 Principles From The Heat Of Faith

Whispers of Hope: Inspiring Stories of Men's Prayers In Scripture

Frontier Legends: The Oregon Dream

Elijah: A Beacon Of Boldness

HOOK, LINE & SAVIOUR - Faith Reflections from Fishing

Driven By Faith: Motor Racing Inspired Christian Life

30 Day Devotional - Bold and Strong- Coffee Devotions for a Courageous Christian Walk

Authentic Christianity: The Heart of Old Time Religion

Consider The Ant - God's Tiny Preachers

Flee Fornication: The Plea For Purity

Renewed Hope- How to Find Encouragement in God

Sounding The Call - The Voice of Conviction

The Altar - Where Heaven Meets Earth

The Bible's Battlefields- Timeless Lessons from Ancient Wars

The Sacred Art of Silence - How Silence Speaks in Scripture

Under Fire- The Sanctity of the Traditional Biblical Home

Who Is on the Lord's Side? A Call to Righteousness

What Is Truth? - From Skepticism to Submission

First and Goal- Faith and Football Fundamentals

From Dugout to Devotion- Spiritual Lessons from Baseball

Par for the Course- Faith and Fairways

The Believer's Pace- Tools for Running Life's Marathon

Introduction

"Anchored in Truth: Exploring the Depths of Psalm 119" is a journey through one of the most profound and comprehensive passages in the Bible, offering a deep exploration of faith, devotion, and the life-transforming power of God's Word. Psalm 119, the longest chapter in the Bible, is a masterpiece of spiritual expression, composed as an intricate acrostic with each section beginning with a letter from the Hebrew alphabet. This psalm is not merely a collection of verses; it is a profound meditation on the beauty, necessity, and all-encompassing nature of God's law. Throughout its 176 verses, the psalmist expresses a fervent love for God's commandments, a deep dependence on His guidance, and a relentless pursuit of understanding and wisdom that only the Scriptures can provide.

In "Anchored in Truth," you will be invited to dive into the rich themes of Psalm 119, each one offering a unique perspective on how God's Word can shape, guide, and sustain a life of faith. This book is designed to help you not only understand the words of this ancient psalm but to experience them in a way that profoundly impacts your daily walk with God. As we explore each section, we will see how the psalmist's words resonate with the challenges and triumphs of our own spiritual journeys. Whether it is seeking deliverance in times of trial, finding delight in God's statutes, or pleading for divine guidance and understanding, the psalmist's experiences echo the realities of our lives today.

This book is not just an intellectual study; it is an invitation to transformation. Psalm 119 calls us to anchor our lives in the unchanging truth of God's Word, to let it be the foundation upon which we build our character, make our decisions, and find our ultimate hope and joy. The psalmist's devotion to God's law is a powerful reminder that Scripture is not just a set of rules or a historical document; it is the living Word of God, active and relevant in every aspect of our lives. As we journey through this psalm, we will discover the depth of God's wisdom and the breadth of His love, both of which are fully revealed in the Scriptures.

"Anchored in Truth" aims to inspire you to cultivate a deeper love for God's Word, to seek His guidance in all things, and to commit to a life that reflects the truth of Scripture. Each chapter will explore the key themes of Psalm 119, providing practical insights and applications that will help you live out the truths found in these verses. Whether you are a seasoned believer looking to deepen your faith or someone new to exploring the Bible, this book will guide you in understanding how to make God's Word the central, defining influence in your life.

As you read " Anchored in Truth: Exploring the Depths of Psalm 119," may you be encouraged to stand firm in the faith, anchored in the unshakeable truths of God's Word, and may your life be transformed by the wisdom, peace, and joy that come from living in alignment with His eternal commands.

Chapter 1 – The Dedication

In Psalm 119, verses 1-8. we find a powerful expression of the psalmist's dedication to walking in the law of the Lord and seeking Him with a whole heart. These verses set the tone for the entire psalm, emphasizing the importance of a deep, unwavering commitment to God's commandments as the foundation of a blessed and righteous life. The psalmist begins with a profound declaration: "Blessed are the undefiled in the way, who walk in the law of the Lord." This opening statement immediately establishes the central theme of dedication to God's law, identifying those who are "undefiled in the way" as blessed—those who live in a manner that is pure, blameless, and in full accordance with the divine commandments. The phrase "walk in the law of the Lord" suggests a continuous, ongoing effort to live according to God's instructions, not merely in moments of convenience or when it suits one's needs, but as a lifelong pursuit. This verse challenges us to consider the extent of our own dedication to God's law. Do we strive to walk in His ways consistently, allowing His Word to guide our every step, or do we sometimes stray from the path, allowing our own desires or the pressures of the world to lead us astray?

The psalmist continues in verse 2, "Blessed are they that keep his testimonies, and that seek him with the whole heart." Here, the psalmist reiterates the blessing that comes from keeping God's testimonies—His decrees and instructions—and emphasizes the necessity of seeking God with a whole heart. The term "whole heart" implies complete sincerity, devotion, and focus, leaving no room for half-heartedness or divided loyalties. To seek God with the whole heart means to prioritize Him above all else, to make Him the center of one's life and the primary object of one's desire. This verse challenges us to examine our own hearts and consider whether we are truly seeking God with all that we are. Are we fully dedicated to pursuing a relationship with Him, or do we allow other interests, distractions, and concerns to take precedence over our devotion to the Lord?

In verse 3, the psalmist describes the behavior of those who are dedicated to God: "They also do no iniquity: they walk in his ways." This verse reinforces the idea that dedication to God involves not only a commitment to following His commandments but also a conscious effort to avoid sin and iniquity. The phrase "do no iniquity" suggests a deliberate choice to live righteously, to resist temptation, and to reject actions that are contrary to God's will. Walking in God's ways, therefore, requires both positive action—following His law—and negative action—refraining from sin. This verse challenges us to consider how we approach the concept of holiness in our own lives. Are we actively striving to do what is right and to avoid what is wrong, recognizing that true dedication to God requires both? Or do we sometimes allow ourselves to compromise, rationalizing our actions or excusing our failures?

The psalmist continues in verse 4 with a statement of divine expectation: "Thou hast commanded us to keep thy precepts diligently." This verse highlights the seriousness of God's commandments and the responsibility that comes with them. The word "diligently" emphasizes the need for careful, consistent, and persistent effort in obeying God's precepts. This is not a casual or occasional commitment; it is an all-encompassing dedication that requires constant attention and effort. The psalmist acknowledges that God's commands are not suggestions or optional guidelines; they are imperatives that must be followed with diligence and precision. This verse challenges us to reflect on our own approach to obedience. Do we take God's commands seriously, striving to keep them with diligence, or do we sometimes treat them as optional, following them when it is convenient or easy but neglecting them when it requires sacrifice or effort?

In verse 5, the psalmist expresses a heartfelt desire for greater dedication: "O that my ways were directed to keep thy statutes!" This verse reveals the psalmist's awareness of his own limitations and weaknesses, and his longing for divine guidance and strength to help him stay true to God's statutes. The phrase "O that my ways were directed" suggests a recognition that without God's help, the psalmist's efforts to live according to His law may falter. This verse is a humble prayer for divine assistance, a plea for God's direction and support in the pursuit of a life dedicated to His commandments. It challenges us to acknowledge our own need for God's guidance and to seek His help in our efforts to live according to His will. Do we recognize that we cannot achieve true holiness and dedication on our own, but must rely on God's grace and strength to guide us?

The psalmist continues in verse 6 with a statement of confidence: "Then shall I not be ashamed, when I have respect unto all thy commandments." This verse expresses the psalmist's belief that by faithfully following God's commandments, he will avoid the shame and disgrace that come from disobedience and sin. The phrase "when I have respect unto all thy commandments" suggests a comprehensive and wholehearted commitment to God's law, not picking and choosing which commandments to follow, but respecting and obeying them all. The psalmist understands that true dedication requires a full embrace of God's Word, with no room for selective obedience or compromise. This verse challenges us to consider whether we are fully committed to following all of God's commandments, or if there are areas of our lives where we are tempted to compromise or ignore certain aspects of His law. Do we strive to live in a way that is consistent with all of God's commands, recognizing that true dedication leaves no room for partial obedience?

In verse 7, the psalmist expresses a desire to praise God through understanding: "I will praise thee with uprightness of heart, when I shall have learned thy righteous judgments." This verse highlights the connection between understanding God's righteous judgments and offering Him genuine praise. The phrase "uprightness of heart" suggests a purity of intention and a sincerity of devotion, indicating that true praise comes from a heart that is fully aligned with God's will. The psalmist recognizes that as he grows in his understanding of God's judgments—His wise and just decisions—his ability to praise God with a sincere and upright heart will also increase. This verse challenges us to consider the relationship between our understanding of God's Word and our ability to worship Him in spirit and truth. Do we seek to deepen our knowledge of God's righteous judgments, knowing that this understanding will enhance our ability to offer Him genuine praise? Or do we sometimes offer praise that is superficial or lacking in true understanding?

The psalmist concludes this section with a vow of dedication in verse 8: "I will keep thy statutes: O forsake me not utterly." This verse encapsulates the psalmist's deep commitment to obeying God's statutes, coupled with a humble acknowledgment of his dependence on God's presence and support. The phrase "I will keep thy statutes" is a declaration of the psalmist's determination to live according to God's law, while the plea "O forsake me not utterly" reflects a recognition of his need for God's continued guidance and grace. The psalmist understands that his ability to keep God's statutes is not something he can achieve on his own; it requires God's ongoing presence and support. This verse challenges us to make a similar commitment to God's commandments in our own lives, while also acknowledging our need for His help and grace. Do we vow to keep God's statutes with the understanding that we must rely on His strength and presence to fulfill that vow? Or do we sometimes attempt to live according to God's law in our own strength, only to falter and fail?

As we explore the theme of dedication in Psalm 119, verses 1-8, we are reminded of the importance of a wholehearted commitment to God's Word in every aspect of our lives. The psalmist's example challenges us to examine the depth of our own dedication to God's commandments, to consider whether we are truly seeking Him with all our heart, and to recognize the need for God's guidance and strength in our pursuit of righteousness. These verses invite us to reflect on our relationship with God's Word and to renew our commitment to walking in His ways with diligence, sincerity, and unwavering devotion. Whether we are facing challenges, seeking to grow in our faith, or striving to live a life that honors God, may we always turn to His Word as our source of strength, guidance, and inspiration, knowing that true dedication to His commandments is the key to a blessed and fulfilling life.

The psalmist's dedication to God's law, as expressed in these verses, serves as a powerful reminder that our commitment to God's Word must be all-encompassing, guiding our every thought, action, and decision. As we continue to meditate on the depth and richness of Psalm 119, may we be inspired to cultivate a similar dedication in our own lives, recognizing that true holiness and righteousness are found in a life that is fully aligned with God's will. Whether we are seeking to grow in our understanding of God's Word, facing the temptations and challenges of the world, or striving to live a life that reflects God's holiness, may we always turn to His Word as our anchor, our guide, and our source of strength, knowing that it is through our dedication to His commandments that we find true joy, peace, and fulfillment. As we journey through the verses of Psalm 119, may we be encouraged to deepen our commitment to God's Word, to seek Him with all our heart, and to walk in His ways with unwavering dedication, trusting that He will guide us, sustain us, and lead us into the fullness of life that He has promised.

Chapter 2 – The Direction

In Psalm 119, verses 9-16, the theme of direction is vividly expressed as the psalmist seeks guidance from God's Word to live a pure and righteous life. These verses reflect a deep longing to walk in the ways of the Lord, recognizing that only through the wisdom and instruction found in Scripture can one navigate the complexities and challenges of life with integrity and holiness. The psalmist begins with a profound question in verse 9: "Wherewithal shall a young man cleanse his way? by taking heed thereto according to thy word." This opening inquiry sets the stage for the entire passage, as the psalmist contemplates the means by which a person, particularly a young man facing the temptations and trials of youth, can maintain a life of purity. The answer is clear and direct: it is by taking heed to God's Word, by aligning one's life with the commandments and principles laid out in Scripture, that one can cleanse their way and live righteously. This verse challenges us to reflect on our own lives and consider how we seek direction and guidance. Do we turn to God's Word as our primary source of wisdom, allowing it to shape our thoughts, actions, and decisions, or do we rely on our own understanding or the shifting standards of the world?

As the psalmist continues in verse 10, he expresses a deep commitment to seeking God with all his heart: "With my whole heart have I sought thee: O let me not wander from thy commandments." This verse highlights the importance of wholehearted devotion in the pursuit of a righteous life. The phrase "with my whole heart" signifies complete and undivided attention, a total dedication to seeking God's will and His direction in every aspect of life. The psalmist's plea, "O let me not wander from thy commandments," reflects a humble acknowledgment of the human tendency to stray from the path of righteousness, and a heartfelt desire to remain steadfast in obedience to God's laws. This verse challenges us to examine the sincerity and intensity of our own pursuit of God. Are we seeking Him with our whole heart, fully committed to following His commandments, or are we allowing distractions, temptations, and worldly influences to pull us away from the path He has set before us?

In verse 11, the psalmist reveals the secret to staying on the right path: "Thy word have I hid in mine heart, that I might not sin against thee." This verse emphasizes the importance of internalizing God's Word, of making it a part of the very fabric of our being. The phrase "hid in mine heart" suggests a deep, personal commitment to memorizing and meditating on Scripture, so that it becomes a guiding force in every decision and action. The psalmist understands that by embedding God's Word in his heart, he can resist the temptations that lead to sin and stay true to God's commandments. This verse challenges us to consider how deeply we have internalized God's Word in our own lives. Have we taken the time to memorize and meditate on Scripture, allowing it to shape our thoughts and actions, or do we only turn to it in times of need, when we are already struggling with temptation or confusion?

The psalmist continues in verse 12 with an expression of praise and a plea for further instruction: "Blessed art thou, O Lord: teach me thy statutes." This verse reflects the psalmist's recognition of God's goodness and the desire to continue growing in understanding and obedience. The phrase "Blessed art thou, O Lord" is an acknowledgment of God's greatness and worthiness of praise, while the plea "teach me thy statutes" reveals a humble dependence on God for guidance and direction. The psalmist understands that true wisdom and understanding come from God alone, and he is eager to learn more of His ways so that he can live in accordance with His will. This verse challenges us to cultivate a similar attitude of praise and humility in our own pursuit of God's direction. Do we recognize God as the ultimate source of wisdom and eagerly seek His instruction, or do we sometimes rely on our own knowledge and understanding, neglecting the need for ongoing learning and growth in our spiritual lives?

In verse 13, the psalmist expresses a commitment to sharing the wisdom he has gained from God's Word: "With my lips have I declared all the judgments of thy mouth." This verse highlights the importance of not only internalizing God's Word but also proclaiming it to others. The phrase "with my lips" indicates that the psalmist is actively speaking about God's judgments—His righteous decisions and commandments—to those around him. This act of declaration serves as a testimony to the psalmist's faith and dedication to God's Word, as well as a means of encouraging others to seek God's direction in their own lives. This verse challenges us to consider how we share the wisdom and guidance we have received from God's Word with others. Are we willing to speak boldly about God's commandments and judgments, sharing the truth of Scripture with those around us, or do we keep it to ourselves, missing opportunities to encourage and guide others in their walk with the Lord?

The psalmist continues in verse 14 with a declaration of delight in God's Word: "I have rejoiced in the way of thy testimonies, as much as in all riches." This verse reveals the psalmist's deep love and appreciation for God's commandments, valuing them more highly than material wealth. The phrase "as much as in all riches" suggests that the psalmist finds as much, if not more, joy and satisfaction in following God's testimonies as others might find in accumulating wealth. This verse challenges us to reflect on what we truly value in life. Do we, like the psalmist, find our greatest joy and fulfillment in living according to God's Word, or do we place higher value on material possessions, success, or the approval of others?

In verse 15, the psalmist further emphasizes his commitment to meditating on God's Word: "I will meditate in thy precepts, and have respect unto thy ways." This verse highlights the importance of regular and intentional reflection on God's commandments as a means of staying aligned with His will. The phrase "meditate in thy precepts" suggests a deep, thoughtful engagement with Scripture, taking the time to ponder its meaning and implications for one's life. The psalmist's commitment to "have respect unto thy ways" indicates a conscious effort to live in a manner that honors God's commandments and reflects His character. This verse challenges us to consider how we approach the study and application of God's Word in our own lives. Do we take the time to meditate on Scripture, allowing it to shape our thoughts, attitudes, and actions, or do we rush through our study, treating it as a task to be completed rather than a means of drawing closer to God?

The passage concludes in verse 16 with a vow of steadfast devotion: "I will delight myself in thy statutes: I will not forget thy word." This final verse encapsulates the psalmist's deep commitment to finding joy in God's commandments and remaining faithful to His Word. The phrase "delight myself in thy statutes" reflects a genuine love for God's law, seeing it not as a burden but as a source of joy and fulfillment. The psalmist's vow to "not forget thy word" underscores the importance of continual remembrance and application of Scripture in every aspect of life. This verse challenges us to reflect on our own attitude toward God's commandments. Do we find delight in following His statutes, seeing them as a source of joy and guidance, or do we sometimes view them as restrictive or burdensome? Are we committed to keeping God's Word at the forefront of our minds, allowing it to guide our decisions and actions, or do we sometimes neglect it, allowing other priorities to take its place?

As we explore the theme of direction in Psalm 119, verses 9-16, we are reminded of the importance of seeking guidance and wisdom from God's Word in every aspect of our lives. The psalmist's example challenges us to consider how we approach the pursuit of a righteous and pure life. Do we, like the psalmist, turn to Scripture as our primary source of direction, allowing it to shape our thoughts, actions, and decisions? Are we committed to seeking God with our whole heart, internalizing His Word, and sharing its wisdom with others?

Furthermore, the psalmist's deep love for God's commandments and his commitment to meditating on them regularly challenges us to examine the depth of our own engagement with Scripture. Are we willing to invest the time and effort required to truly understand and apply God's Word in our lives, recognizing that it is through this process that we receive the direction and guidance we need to live according to His will?

In conclusion, the theme of direction in Psalm 119, verses 9-16, offers a powerful reminder of the importance of grounding our lives in the truth and wisdom of God's Word. The psalmist's deep commitment to seeking direction from Scripture, his desire to internalize God's commandments, and his dedication to sharing and meditating on God's Word challenge us to anchor our lives in the unchanging truth of Scripture. As we continue to explore the depths of Psalm 119, may we be inspired to seek God's direction in every aspect of our lives, recognizing that it is through His Word that we find the wisdom, guidance, and strength we need to navigate the complexities and challenges of life.

Whether we are seeking to grow in our understanding of God's Word, facing difficult decisions, or striving to live a life that honors God, may we always turn to His Word as our source of direction and guidance, knowing that it is through our dedication to His commandments that we find the path to true righteousness and peace. The psalmist's example reminds us that true discernment and direction come not from our own understanding or the shifting standards of the world, but from the eternal and unchanging truth of God's Word. By placing our trust in God's Word and seeking His guidance in every aspect of our lives, we can experience the peace, strength, and fulfillment that come from living a life that is anchored in the truth of His commandments. As we continue to journey through Psalm 119, may we be encouraged to deepen our commitment to seeking God's direction through His Word, finding in it the wisdom and guidance we need to navigate the challenges and joys of life, anchored in the truth of God's Word.

Chapter 3 – The Delight

In Psalm 119, verses 17-24, the theme of delight emerges as the psalmist expresses profound joy and satisfaction in God's statutes, even while facing scorn and oppression. These verses convey the deep comfort and strength that come from anchoring one's life in the unchanging truth of God's Word, highlighting how delighting in His commandments can sustain and uplift us through the most challenging circumstances. The psalmist begins in verse 17 with a plea for God's favor: "Deal bountifully with thy servant, that I may live, and keep thy word." This opening verse sets the tone for the passage, reflecting a deep dependence on God's grace and a desire to live in accordance with His Word. The psalmist recognizes that life itself, with all its meaning and purpose, is intimately tied to the ability to keep God's commandments. The phrase "deal bountifully" suggests a longing for God's generous blessing, not for selfish gain, but so that the psalmist may continue to faithfully follow His Word. This verse challenges us to consider our own motivations for seeking God's favor. Do we desire His blessings so that we might live more fully in obedience to His Word, or do we seek His favor for personal gain, neglecting the higher purpose of glorifying Him through our lives?

In verse 18, the psalmist continues with a heartfelt request for spiritual insight: "Open thou mine eyes, that I may behold wondrous things out of thy law." This verse highlights the psalmist's understanding that the ability to truly see and appreciate the depth of God's law requires divine intervention. The phrase "open thou mine eyes" indicates that the psalmist is aware of his own limitations and the need for God to reveal the deeper truths embedded in His Word. The "wondrous things" that the psalmist longs to behold are the profound and life-changing insights that can only be discerned through a heart and mind illuminated by the Holy Spirit. This verse challenges us to approach God's Word with humility and a recognition that we need

God's help to truly understand and delight in His statutes. Are we seeking God's revelation in our study of Scripture, asking Him to open our eyes to the wonders of His law, or are we relying solely on our own intellect and understanding?

The psalmist's sense of alienation in the world is poignantly expressed in verse 19: "I am a stranger in the earth: hide not thy commandments from me." This verse reflects the psalmist's awareness of being out of place in a world that does not share his values or devotion to God's Word. The phrase "a stranger in the earth" suggests a feeling of disconnection or isolation, as if the psalmist is a foreigner in a land where he does not fully belong. This sense of estrangement drives the psalmist to cling even more tightly to God's commandments, recognizing them as his true home and source of identity. The plea "hide not thy commandments from me" reveals a deep longing for God's guidance and presence in a world that often feels hostile and alienating. This verse challenges us to reflect on our own experiences of feeling like strangers in a world that is increasingly at odds with God's truth. Do we, like the psalmist, turn to God's commandments as our anchor and source of comfort, or do we allow the pressures and values of the world to lead us away from our true home in God's Word?

In verse 20, the psalmist expresses an intense longing for God's judgments: "My soul breaketh for the longing that it hath unto thy judgments at all times." This verse reveals the psalmist's deep, almost overwhelming desire for God's righteous decrees. The phrase "my soul breaketh" conveys a sense of intense yearning, as if the psalmist's very being is consumed with a desire to know and live by God's judgments. This longing is not sporadic or occasional; it is a constant and enduring passion, reflecting a heart that is fully devoted to God's Word. This verse challenges us to consider the depth of our own desire for God's truth. Are we, like the psalmist, deeply and consistently longing for God's judgments, allowing that desire to shape every aspect of our lives, or do we approach God's Word with a more casual or indifferent attitude?

The psalmist's awareness of the opposition he faces is evident in verse 21: "Thou hast rebuked the proud that are cursed, which do err from thy commandments." This verse acknowledges the reality of those who are proud and self-sufficient, who have turned away from God's commandments and are consequently under His rebuke. The psalmist recognizes that the proud, those who refuse to submit to God's authority, are not only in error but are also cursed—separated from the blessings that come from living in obedience to God's Word. This verse highlights the psalmist's understanding of the serious consequences of straying from God's commandments, both for himself and for those who oppose him. It challenges us to reflect on how we respond to the proud and disobedient in our own lives. Do we, like the psalmist, remain committed to God's judgments, recognizing the dangers of pride and disobedience, or are we tempted to follow the ways of those who reject God's truth?

In verse 22, the psalmist pleads for deliverance from reproach and contempt: "Remove from me reproach and contempt; for I have kept thy testimonies." This verse reveals the psalmist's deep sensitivity to the scorn and derision he faces from others, likely because of his unwavering commitment to God's commandments. The phrases "reproach and contempt" indicate the harsh judgments and disrespect he endures, but rather than retaliate or abandon his principles, the psalmist turns to God for vindication. The psalmist's plea is based on his faithfulness to God's testimonies, suggesting that he sees his adherence to God's Word as a defense against the unjust accusations of others. This verse challenges us to consider how we respond to criticism and opposition in our own lives. Do we, like the psalmist, remain steadfast in our commitment to God's Word, trusting Him to remove reproach and contempt, or do we allow the opinions of others to shake our faith and lead us away from our convictions?

The psalmist's determination to remain focused on God's statutes, despite opposition, is further emphasized in verse 23: "Princes also did sit and speak against me: but thy servant did meditate in thy statutes." This verse highlights the psalmist's resilience and steadfastness in the face of powerful opposition. The mention of "princes" suggests that those in positions of authority and influence are speaking against the psalmist, likely trying to undermine his reputation or influence. However, rather than be swayed or intimidated by their words, the psalmist chooses to meditate on God's statutes, finding strength and guidance in the truth of God's Word. This verse challenges us to reflect on how we respond to the criticisms or attacks of those in authority or with influence in our own lives. Do we, like the psalmist, choose to meditate on God's Word, allowing it to guide our responses and actions, or do we succumb to fear or pressure, compromising our principles in the face of opposition?

The passage concludes in verse 24 with a declaration of the psalmist's delight in God's testimonies: "Thy testimonies also are my delight and my counsellors." This final verse encapsulates the deep joy and satisfaction the psalmist finds in God's Word, describing it as both his delight and his source of counsel. The phrase "my delight" reflects a profound love and appreciation for God's testimonies, seeing them not as burdensome rules, but as a source of joy and fulfillment. The psalmist's reference to God's testimonies as "my counsellors" suggests that he turns to Scripture for guidance and wisdom in every aspect of his life, trusting that God's Word will provide the direction he needs. This verse challenges us to consider the role of God's Word in our own lives. Do we, like the psalmist, find delight in God's testimonies, allowing them to bring us joy and guide our decisions, or do we see them as mere rules or guidelines, lacking in relevance or personal significance?

As we explore the theme of delight in Psalm 119, verses 17-24, we are reminded of the importance of finding joy and comfort in

God's Word, even in the midst of scorn and oppression. The psalmist's example challenges us to consider how we approach God's commandments and judgments. Do we, like the psalmist, delight in God's Word, allowing it to shape our lives and sustain us through difficult times, or do we allow the pressures and criticisms of the world to dampen our joy and weaken our commitment to His truth?

Furthermore, the psalmist's deep longing for God's judgments and his commitment to meditating on Scripture, even in the face of opposition, challenges us to examine the depth of our own engagement with God's Word. Are we willing to invest the time and effort required to truly understand and apply God's testimonies in our lives, recognizing that they are the source of true wisdom, guidance, and delight?

In conclusion, the theme of delight in Psalm 119, verses 17-24, offers a powerful reminder of the joy and comfort that come from anchoring our lives in the truth of God's Word. The psalmist's deep love for God's commandments, his commitment to meditating on them regularly, and his resilience in the face of opposition challenge us to anchor our lives in the unchanging truth of Scripture. As we continue to explore the depths of Psalm 119, may we be inspired to find our delight in God's Word, recognizing that it is through our dedication to His commandments that we find the strength, guidance, and comfort we need to navigate the challenges and joys of life.

Whether we are facing criticism, seeking to grow in our understanding of God's Word, or striving to live a life that honors God, may we always turn to His Word as our source of delight and counsel, knowing that it is through our love for His testimonies that we find true peace and fulfillment. The psalmist's example reminds us that true joy and satisfaction come not from the approval of others or the accumulation of worldly success, but from a deep and abiding relationship with God through His Word. By placing our trust in God's Word and seeking His guidance in every aspect of our lives, we can experience the joy, peace, and fulfillment that come from living a life that is anchored in the truth of His commandments. As we continue to journey through Psalm 119, may we be encouraged to deepen our commitment to finding delight in God's Word, allowing it to bring us comfort, strength, and joy, even in the midst of life's challenges, anchored in the truth of God's eternal Word.

Chapter 4 – The Dependence

In Psalm 119, verses 25-32, the theme of dependence is poignantly explored as the psalmist turns to God's Word for revival and strength during times of deep sorrow and affliction. These verses convey a powerful sense of vulnerability and need, highlighting the psalmist's recognition that, in moments of despair, it is only through reliance on God's eternal Word that one can find the hope, renewal, and courage necessary to persevere. The psalmist begins in verse 25 with a cry from the depths of his soul: "My soul cleaveth unto the dust: quicken thou me according to thy word." This opening verse captures the intensity of the psalmist's suffering, as he describes his soul clinging to the dust, a metaphor for extreme lowliness, despair, and even proximity to death. The word "cleaveth" suggests that the psalmist feels utterly weighed down by his afflictions, almost as if he is being pulled into the earth by the gravity of his sorrow. Yet, even in this desperate state, the psalmist turns to God with a plea for revival—"quicken thou me"—asking God to breathe life back into his weary soul. Importantly, the psalmist does not seek revival through his own efforts or worldly means but depends entirely on the power of God's Word, asking for renewal "according to thy word." This verse challenges us to reflect on our own sources of strength in times of trouble. Do we, like the psalmist, turn to God's Word as our primary source of life and revitalization when we are overwhelmed by sorrow, or do we attempt to find solace in temporary or superficial solutions that ultimately fail to satisfy?

As the psalmist continues in verse 26, he confesses his struggles and seeks God's guidance: "I have declared my ways, and thou heardest me: teach me thy statutes." This verse reflects the psalmist's openness and honesty with God, as he lays bare his thoughts, actions, and the paths he has taken. The phrase "declared my ways" suggests that the psalmist has poured out his heart before God, acknowledging his weaknesses, failures, and the confusion that may have led him astray. Yet, the psalmist finds comfort in the knowledge that God has heard him—"thou heardest me"—and responds to his plea for understanding by asking God to "teach me thy statutes." This request for divine instruction indicates the psalmist's recognition that his own understanding is insufficient and that he must rely on God's Word to find the right path forward. This verse challenges us to consider how we approach our relationship with God, especially in times of distress. Are we willing to be completely transparent with God, confessing our struggles and seeking His guidance through Scripture, or do we try to navigate our difficulties on our own, without fully acknowledging our need for His wisdom?

In verse 27, the psalmist expresses a desire for deeper understanding: "Make me to understand the way of thy precepts: so shall I talk of thy wondrous works." This verse highlights the psalmist's longing for insight into the deeper meanings of God's commandments. The phrase "make me to understand" suggests that the psalmist recognizes that true comprehension of God's Word requires divine enlightenment—it is not something that can be fully grasped through human effort alone. The psalmist's desire for understanding is not merely intellectual; it is deeply practical, as it is linked to his ability to "talk of thy wondrous works." The psalmist wants to understand God's precepts so that he can share the truth and beauty of God's works with others, thereby bringing glory to God. This verse challenges us to reflect on our own pursuit of understanding. Do we seek to comprehend God's Word so that we might live according to His will and share His truth with others, or is our study of Scripture superficial, lacking the depth of insight that comes from truly depending on God for understanding?

The psalmist's expression of sorrow intensifies in verse 28: "My soul melteth for heaviness: strengthen thou me according unto thy word." This verse vividly portrays the weight of the psalmist's grief, as he describes his soul melting under the burden of his sorrow. The word "melteth" conveys a sense of being overwhelmed, as if the psalmist's very being is dissolving under the pressure of his afflictions. Yet, even in this state of profound despair, the psalmist turns to God for strength, asking to be upheld "according unto thy word." This plea reflects the psalmist's deep dependence on God's promises and the sustaining power of Scripture. The psalmist understands that his strength does not come from within but is derived from the truth and assurance found in God's Word. This verse challenges us to consider where we turn for strength when we are weighed down by grief and hardship. Do we, like the psalmist, rely on God's Word to sustain us, trusting that His promises will provide the strength we need to endure, or do we try to muster strength from within, only to find ourselves exhausted and defeated?

In verse 29, the psalmist seeks deliverance from deceit and a commitment to truth: "Remove from me the way of lying: and grant me thy law graciously." This verse reveals the psalmist's recognition of the dangers of falsehood and the importance of living in accordance with God's truth. The phrase "remove from me the way of lying" indicates a desire to be freed from any inclination toward deceit, whether it is self-deception, dishonesty with others, or being misled by the lies of the world. The psalmist understands that living a life of integrity and truth requires God's intervention, and so he asks for God's law to be granted to him "graciously." This request for grace highlights the psalmist's awareness that adherence to God's law is not something that can be achieved through human effort alone; it requires God's merciful assistance. This verse challenges us to examine our own commitment to truth. Do we, like the psalmist, seek God's help in turning away from deceit and embracing His truth, or do we sometimes allow falsehoods to take root in our lives, whether through intentional dishonesty or by accepting the lies of the world?

The psalmist's resolve to follow God's truth is further emphasized in verse 30: "I have chosen the way of truth: thy judgments have I laid before me." This verse reflects a deliberate and conscious decision to live according to God's truth. The phrase "I have chosen the way of truth" indicates that the psalmist has made a definitive choice to reject falsehood and embrace the path of righteousness. By laying God's judgments "before me," the psalmist is declaring his intention to keep God's commandments always in view, using them as a guide for every decision and action. This verse challenges us to consider the choices we make in our own lives. Are we, like the psalmist, consciously choosing to follow the way of truth, keeping God's Word at the forefront of our minds, or do we sometimes drift into paths of compromise and falsehood, neglecting the guidance of Scripture?

In verse 31, the psalmist reiterates his dependence on God's Word as a source of strength and stability: "I have stuck unto thy testimonies: O Lord, put me not to shame." This verse conveys the psalmist's unwavering commitment to clinging to God's testimonies, despite the challenges and pressures he faces. The phrase "I have stuck unto thy testimonies" suggests a tenacious grip on God's Word, refusing to let go even when circumstances are difficult or when others might mock or scorn him for his faith. The psalmist's plea, "O Lord, put me not to shame," reflects a deep desire for God's vindication, trusting that by remaining faithful to God's Word, he will not be disappointed or disgraced. This verse challenges us to examine our own steadfastness in holding onto God's Word. Do we, like the psalmist, cling to Scripture as our anchor, trusting that God will uphold us and protect us from shame, or do we sometimes waver in our commitment, especially when faced with ridicule or opposition?

The passage concludes in verse 32 with a declaration of the psalmist's eagerness to follow God's commandments: "I will run the way of thy commandments, when thou shalt enlarge my heart." This verse captures the psalmist's enthusiasm and determination to live according to God's Word. The phrase "I will run" suggests not just a willingness, but a fervent eagerness to obey God's commandments, as if the psalmist is ready to pursue the path of righteousness with all his might. The request for God to "enlarge my heart" indicates a desire for greater capacity to love, understand, and follow God's law. The psalmist recognizes that in order to fully embrace God's commandments, he needs God to expand his heart, to increase his ability to live in accordance with His will. This verse challenges us to consider our own enthusiasm for following God's commandments. Are we, like the psalmist, eager to run the way of God's commandments, asking God to enlarge our hearts so that we might love and obey Him more fully, or do we approach obedience with reluctance, feeling constrained or burdened by His laws?

As we explore the theme of dependence in Psalm 119, verses 25-32, we are reminded of the importance of relying on God's Word for strength, guidance, and renewal, especially in times of sorrow and affliction. The psalmist's example challenges us to consider how we approach our relationship with God's Word in moments of distress. Do we, like the psalmist, turn to Scripture

as our primary source of life and revival, trusting in its power to sustain us, or do we seek comfort and solutions elsewhere, only to find ourselves still longing for the peace that only God's Word can provide?

Furthermore, the psalmist's commitment to truth, his rejection of falsehood, and his resolve to follow God's commandments with eagerness and determination challenge us to examine the depth of our own dependence on God's Word. Are we willing to be fully transparent with God, confessing our struggles and seeking His guidance through Scripture? Do we consciously choose the way of truth, clinging to God's testimonies even when faced with opposition or ridicule? And are we eager to run the way of God's commandments, asking Him to enlarge our hearts so that we might love and obey Him more fully?

In conclusion, the theme of dependence in Psalm 119, verses 25-32, offers a powerful reminder of the need to anchor our lives in the truth and strength of God's Word, especially in times of deep sorrow and affliction. The psalmist's deep reliance on Scripture, his commitment to living according to God's truth, and his fervent desire for God's guidance challenge us to anchor our lives in the unchanging truth of Scripture. As we continue to explore the depths of Psalm 119, may we be inspired to deepen our dependence on God's Word, recognizing that it is through His Word that we find the strength, renewal, and guidance we need to navigate the challenges and sorrows of life.

Whether we are facing grief, seeking to grow in our understanding of God's Word, or striving to live a life that honors God, may we always turn to His Word as our source of strength and direction, knowing that it is through our dependence on His commandments that we find the path to true revival and peace. The psalmist's example reminds us that true strength and renewal come not from within ourselves or from the world around us, but from the life-giving power of God's Word. By placing our trust in God's Word and seeking His guidance in every aspect of our lives, we can experience the peace, strength, and fulfillment that come from living a life that is anchored in the truth of His commandments. As we continue to journey through Psalm 119, may we be encouraged to deepen our commitment to depending on God's Word, finding in it the strength, renewal, and guidance we need to navigate the challenges and joys of life, anchored in the truth of God's eternal Word.

Chapter 5 – The Desire

In Psalm 119, verses 33-40, the theme of desire is vividly explored as the psalmist expresses a fervent longing to understand and follow God's commandments, pleading for life that aligns with God's righteousness. These verses capture the intensity of the psalmist's yearning to live in obedience to God's laws, recognizing that true life, wisdom, and fulfillment are found in unwavering commitment to His Word. The psalmist begins in verse 33 with a heartfelt request: "Teach me, O Lord, the way of thy statutes; and I shall keep it unto the end." This opening plea reflects the psalmist's deep desire not only to know God's commandments but also to be faithful in keeping them throughout his life. The phrase "unto the end" emphasizes the psalmist's commitment to lifelong obedience, underscoring the idea that following God's statutes is not a temporary or superficial endeavor but a lifelong pursuit. This verse challenges us to examine the depth of our own desire to follow God's commandments. Are we, like the psalmist, eager to be taught by God, with a commitment to keeping His statutes faithfully for the rest of our lives, or do we sometimes approach obedience as a short-term goal, easily swayed by changing circumstances or temptations?

As the psalmist continues in verse 34, he expresses a longing for understanding: "Give me understanding, and I shall keep thy law; yea, I shall observe it with my whole heart." This verse highlights the psalmist's recognition that true obedience to God's law requires more than just knowledge; it requires understanding. The phrase "give me understanding" suggests that the psalmist is aware of his own limitations and the need for divine insight to fully grasp the meaning and implications of God's commandments. The commitment to observe the law "with my whole heart" further emphasizes the psalmist's desire to follow God's commandments with complete sincerity and devotion. This verse challenges us to consider how we approach the study and application of God's Word. Do we, like the psalmist, seek understanding that goes beyond surface-level knowledge, desiring to observe God's law with our whole heart, or do we sometimes settle for a shallow or partial understanding of Scripture, lacking the depth of insight that leads to wholehearted obedience?

In verse 35, the psalmist continues his plea for divine guidance: "Make me to go in the path of thy commandments; for therein do I delight." This verse reflects the psalmist's desire not only to understand God's commandments but also to actively walk in the path they set forth. The phrase "make me to go" suggests a recognition that following God's commandments requires more than just a willing heart; it requires God's enabling power. The psalmist's declaration that he delights in God's commandments highlights the joy and fulfillment that come from living in accordance with God's will. This verse challenges us to reflect on our own attitude toward obedience. Do we, like the psalmist, find delight in following God's commandments, asking Him to guide us and empower us to walk in His ways, or do we sometimes view obedience as a burden or obligation, lacking the joy that comes from a deep connection with God's Word?

The psalmist's desire for undivided devotion is expressed in verse 36: "Incline my heart unto thy testimonies, and not to covetousness." This verse reveals the psalmist's awareness of the distractions and temptations that can pull his heart away from God's Word. The phrase "incline my heart" suggests a need for God's intervention to keep the psalmist's desires aligned with His will. By contrasting God's testimonies with covetousness, the psalmist acknowledges the dangers of materialism and the pursuit of worldly gain, which can lead the heart away from God. This verse challenges us to examine where our hearts are inclined. Do we, like the psalmist, ask God to incline our hearts toward His testimonies, seeking to avoid the pitfalls of covetousness and worldly desires, or do we sometimes allow our hearts to be drawn away by the allure of material possessions and earthly success?

In verse 37, the psalmist continues his plea for divine protection against distractions: "Turn away mine eyes from beholding vanity; and quicken thou me in thy way." This verse highlights the psalmist's recognition that the eyes can be gateways to the heart, leading to desires that are vain and empty. The phrase "beholding vanity" suggests an awareness of the superficial and fleeting nature of worldly attractions, which can distract from the pursuit of God's truth. The psalmist's request for God to "quicken" him in His way reflects a desire for spiritual renewal and vitality, recognizing that true life is found in walking according to God's commandments. This verse challenges us to consider what captures our attention and where we direct our focus. Do we, like the psalmist, ask God to turn our eyes away from vanity, seeking instead the life-giving path of His commandments, or do we sometimes find ourselves drawn to things that are ultimately empty and meaningless, detracting from our spiritual growth and relationship with God?

The psalmist's longing for God's confirmation of His Word is evident in verse 38: "Stablish thy word unto thy servant, who is devoted to thy fear." This verse reflects the psalmist's desire for God's promises to be firmly established in his life. The phrase "stablish thy word" suggests a need for assurance and confirmation of God's truth, reinforcing the psalmist's commitment to living in reverence of God—"who is devoted to thy fear." The psalmist's devotion to fearing God indicates a deep respect and awe for God's holiness and authority, which underpins his desire for God's Word to be a solid foundation in his life. This verse challenges us to consider our own commitment to God's Word and His promises. Do we, like the psalmist, seek for God's Word to be established firmly in our lives, living in reverence and devotion to Him, or do we sometimes waver in our commitment, unsure of God's promises and lacking the deep-rooted faith that comes from a life anchored in His Word?

In verse 39, the psalmist seeks deliverance from reproach: "Turn away my reproach which I fear: for thy judgments are good." This verse reveals the psalmist's concern about being shamed or disgraced, particularly in the eyes of others, but it is also a reflection of his deep trust in the goodness of God's judgments. The phrase "turn away my reproach" suggests a plea for God's protection and vindication, ensuring that the psalmist is not dishonored as he strives to live according to God's commandments. The affirmation that "thy judgments are good" underscores the psalmist's confidence in the righteousness and fairness of God's decisions, even when they involve correction or discipline. This verse challenges us to reflect on how we respond to the possibility of reproach or shame in our own lives. Do we, like the psalmist, trust in the goodness of God's judgments, asking Him to protect us from reproach, or do we sometimes allow the fear of others' opinions or judgments to influence our actions, leading us away from obedience to God?

The passage concludes in verse 40 with a powerful expression of desire for God's righteousness: "Behold, I have longed after thy precepts: quicken me in thy righteousness." This final verse encapsulates the psalmist's deep yearning for God's commandments and the life-giving power of His righteousness. The phrase "I have longed after thy precepts" indicates a strong and persistent desire to live according to God's Word, reflecting a heart that is fully devoted to following His commandments. The request for God to "quicken me in thy righteousness" reveals the psalmist's recognition that true life and vitality are found in aligning oneself with God's righteous standards. This verse challenges us to consider the intensity of our own desire for God's precepts and righteousness. Do we, like the psalmist, long for God's commandments with a deep and abiding passion, seeking to be quickened and renewed in His righteousness, or do we sometimes find our desires directed elsewhere, lacking the fervor and commitment that comes from a heart fully devoted to God's Word?

As we explore the theme of desire in Psalm 119, verses 33-40, we are reminded of the importance of cultivating a strong and persistent longing to understand and follow God's commandments. The psalmist's example challenges us to consider how we approach our relationship with God's Word. Do we, like the psalmist, seek divine instruction and understanding with a wholehearted commitment to living according to God's statutes, or do we sometimes approach obedience with a lack of passion or depth, easily swayed by distractions and competing desires?

Furthermore, the psalmist's recognition of the dangers of covetousness, vanity, and reproach, and his plea for God's guidance and protection, challenge us to examine the priorities and influences in our own lives. Are we willing to ask God to incline our hearts toward His testimonies, to turn our eyes away from vanity, and to protect us from reproach as we strive to live in accordance with His Word, or do we sometimes allow worldly desires and fears to dictate our actions, leading us away from the path of righteousness?

In conclusion, the theme of desire in Psalm 119, verses 33-40, offers a powerful reminder of the need to anchor our lives in a deep and abiding longing for God's commandments and His righteousness. The psalmist's fervent prayers for understanding, guidance, and protection, and his unwavering commitment to living according to God's Word, challenge us to cultivate a similar desire in our own lives. As we continue to explore the depths of Psalm 119, may we be inspired to deepen our longing for God's precepts, recognizing that it is through our desire for His commandments and His righteousness that we find true life, wisdom, and fulfillment.

Whether we are seeking to grow in our understanding of God's Word, striving to live a life that honors God, or facing the temptations and distractions of the world, may we always turn to His Word as our source of guidance and renewal, knowing that it is through our desire for His righteousness that we find the strength and direction we need to navigate the challenges and joys of life. The psalmist's example reminds us that true fulfillment and joy come not from the pursuit of worldly desires, but from a deep and persistent longing to live according to God's commandments. By placing our trust in God's Word and seeking His guidance in every aspect of our lives, we can experience the peace, strength, and fulfillment that come from living a life that is anchored in the truth of His commandments. As we continue to journey through Psalm 119, may we be encouraged to deepen our desire for God's Word, finding in it the wisdom, guidance, and life-giving power we need to live a life that is fully devoted to Him, anchored in the truth of God's eternal Word.

Chapter 6 – The Defense

In Psalm 119, verses 41-48, the theme of defense is powerfully explored as the psalmist turns to God's Word as a shield against those who mock and oppress him, while also committing to speak and live according to God's commandments with unwavering dedication. These verses vividly depict the psalmist's reliance on God's Word as his primary means of protection and guidance in the face of adversity, demonstrating how deeply anchored he is in the truth and promises of Scripture. The psalmist begins in verse 41 with a heartfelt plea: "Let thy mercies come also unto me, O Lord, even thy salvation, according to thy word." This opening verse sets the tone for the entire passage, as the psalmist seeks the mercies and salvation of the Lord, not as abstract concepts, but as realities grounded in the promises of God's Word. The use of the phrase "according to thy word" emphasizes the psalmist's trust in the reliability and faithfulness of God's promises. He understands that God's Word is not just a collection of ancient texts but a living, active force that can bring about real deliverance and protection in his life. This verse challenges us to reflect on where we seek our own defense in times of trouble. Do we, like the psalmist, turn to God's Word as the ultimate source of mercy and salvation, trusting in the promises contained within Scripture, or do we seek refuge in worldly solutions that may ultimately prove inadequate?

In verse 42, the psalmist expresses confidence in God's Word as his defense against those who taunt and scorn him: "So shall I have wherewith to answer him that reproacheth me: for I trust in thy word." This verse highlights the psalmist's recognition that God's Word provides him with the strength and wisdom needed to respond to those who mock or criticize him. The phrase "wherewith to answer him" suggests that the psalmist is not left defenseless in the face of reproach; rather, he is equipped with the truth and promises of God's Word, which serve as a powerful retort to those who would undermine his faith. The psalmist's declaration, "for I trust in thy word," underscores the depth of his reliance on Scripture as his primary source of defense. This verse challenges us to consider how we respond to criticism and opposition in our own lives. Do we, like the psalmist, trust in God's Word to provide the answers and strength we need when faced with reproach, or do we allow the opinions of others to shake our confidence and lead us away from our commitment to God's truth?

The psalmist's commitment to God's commandments is further emphasized in verse 43: "And take not the word of truth utterly out of my mouth; for I have hoped in thy judgments." This verse reveals the psalmist's deep desire to continually speak the truth of God's Word, even in the face of opposition. The phrase "take not the word of truth utterly out of my mouth" reflects the psalmist's fear of losing the ability to proclaim God's truth, highlighting the importance he places on being a vocal and active witness to God's commandments. The psalmist's hope in God's judgments underscores his belief that God's decisions and decrees are just and right, providing a solid foundation for his speech and actions. This verse challenges us to examine our own commitment to speaking God's truth. Do we, like the psalmist, strive to keep God's Word on our lips at all times, even when it is difficult or unpopular, or do we sometimes remain silent out of fear of rejection or misunderstanding?

In verse 44, the psalmist reaffirms his lifelong commitment to keeping God's law: "So shall I keep thy law continually for ever and ever." This verse expresses the psalmist's determination to live in obedience to God's commandments, not just for a season, but for all of his days. The use of the phrase "for ever and ever" indicates an eternal perspective, suggesting that the psalmist views his commitment to God's law as something that transcends the temporal challenges he faces. This verse challenges us to consider the permanence of our own commitment to God's commandments. Are we, like the psalmist, dedicated to keeping God's law continually, regardless of the circumstances or the passing of time, or do we allow our commitment to waver in response to changing situations or pressures?

The psalmist's sense of freedom and confidence in God's commandments is beautifully expressed in verse 45: "And I will walk at liberty: for I seek thy precepts." This verse reveals the paradoxical truth that true freedom is found in obedience to God's Word. The phrase "walk at liberty" suggests a life lived in freedom from the constraints and fears imposed by the world, a freedom that comes from seeking and following God's precepts. The psalmist understands that God's commandments are not restrictive or burdensome; rather, they provide the guidance and boundaries necessary for a life of true freedom and fulfillment. This verse challenges us to reflect on our own understanding of freedom. Do we, like the psalmist, recognize that true liberty is found in seeking and obeying God's precepts, or do we sometimes view God's commandments as limiting our freedom, not realizing that they are designed to protect and liberate us?

In verse 46, the psalmist declares his intention to boldly speak of God's commandments, even before those in positions of power: "I will speak of thy testimonies also before kings, and will not be ashamed." This verse highlights the psalmist's courage and determination to proclaim God's truth, regardless of the audience or potential consequences. The phrase "before kings" suggests that the psalmist is willing to speak God's Word even in the presence of those who hold great authority and power, individuals who might be hostile or indifferent to God's commandments. The psalmist's resolve to "not be ashamed" reflects his deep conviction and confidence in the truth of God's testimonies. This verse challenges us to consider our own willingness to speak boldly about our faith. Are we, like the psalmist, ready to proclaim God's truth in any situation, even when faced with powerful opposition, or do we sometimes shrink back out of fear of embarrassment or rejection?

The psalmist's delight in God's commandments is further emphasized in verse 47: "And I will delight myself in thy commandments, which I have loved." This verse reveals the deep joy and affection the psalmist finds in following God's commandments. The phrase "delight myself" indicates that the psalmist does not view God's laws as a burden or obligation, but as a source of joy and fulfillment. The psalmist's love for God's commandments is a recurring theme throughout Psalm 119, highlighting the intimate relationship he has with God's Word. This verse challenges us to reflect on our own attitude toward God's commandments. Do we, like the psalmist, delight in God's Word, finding joy and satisfaction in living according to His precepts, or do we sometimes view obedience as a duty or chore, lacking the deep love and affection that the psalmist expresses?

The passage concludes in verse 48 with a powerful expression of devotion and reverence: "My hands also will I lift up unto thy commandments, which I have loved; and I will meditate in thy statutes." This final verse encapsulates the psalmist's deep commitment to God's Word, both in action and contemplation. The phrase "lift up my hands" is a gesture of worship and surrender, indicating the psalmist's willingness to fully submit to and honor God's commandments. The psalmist's declaration that he will "meditate in thy statutes" underscores the importance of not only following God's laws but also deeply reflecting on them, allowing them to shape his thoughts, attitudes, and actions. This verse challenges us to consider the depth of our own devotion to God's Word. Are we, like the psalmist, willing to lift up our hands in worship and surrender to God's commandments, and to meditate on His statutes with the intention of allowing them to transform our lives, or do we sometimes approach

Scripture superficially, without fully engaging with its profound truths?

As we explore the theme of defense in Psalm 119, verses 41-48, we are reminded of the critical importance of relying on God's Word as our primary source of protection, guidance, and strength in the face of adversity. The psalmist's example challenges us to consider how we approach our relationship with God's Word, especially when confronted with opposition, criticism, or mockery. Do we, like the psalmist, trust in God's Word to be our defense, providing the answers, strength, and courage we need to stand firm in our faith, or do we allow the pressures and opinions of others to undermine our confidence and commitment to God's truth?

Furthermore, the psalmist's deep love for God's commandments, his willingness to speak boldly about his faith, and his commitment to lifelong obedience challenge us to examine the depth of our own devotion to God's Word. Are we willing to speak God's truth, even in the face of powerful opposition? Do we delight in God's commandments, finding joy and satisfaction in living according to His precepts? And are we committed to continually meditating on God's Word, allowing it to shape and guide every aspect of our lives?

In conclusion, the theme of defense in Psalm 119, verses 41-48, offers a powerful reminder of the need to anchor our lives in the truth and strength of God's Word, especially when facing the challenges and opposition of the world. The psalmist's deep reliance on Scripture as his defense, his commitment to speaking and living according to God's commandments, and his unwavering devotion to meditating on God's statutes challenge us to anchor our lives in the unchanging truth of Scripture. As we continue to explore the depths of Psalm 119, may we be inspired to deepen our trust in God's Word, recognizing that it is through our commitment to His commandments that we find the strength, courage, and defense we need to navigate the challenges and joys of life.

Whether we are facing criticism, seeking to grow in our understanding of God's Word, or striving to live a life that honors God, may we always turn to His Word as our source of defense and guidance, knowing that it is through our love for His commandments that we find true peace and fulfillment. The psalmist's example reminds us that true strength and protection come not from our own efforts or from the world around us, but from the life-giving power of God's Word. By placing our trust in God's Word and seeking His guidance in every aspect of our lives, we can experience the peace, strength, and fulfillment that come from living a life that is anchored in the truth of His commandments. As we continue to journey through Psalm 119, may we be encouraged to deepen our commitment to defending and proclaiming God's Word, finding in it the wisdom, guidance, and strength we need to live a life that is fully devoted to Him, anchored in the truth of God's eternal Word.

Chapter 7 – The Determination

In Psalm 119, verses 49-56, the theme of determination is deeply explored as the psalmist resolutely commits to holding onto God's promises and laws, even amidst suffering and derision. These verses highlight the psalmist's unwavering resolve to stay anchored in the truth of God's Word, demonstrating the power of faith and perseverance when facing adversity. The psalmist begins in verse 49 with a plea to God: "Remember the word unto thy servant, upon which thou hast caused me to hope." This opening verse sets the tone for the entire passage, as the psalmist reminds God of His promises, which have been a source of hope and encouragement. The phrase "upon which thou hast caused me to hope" reflects the deep connection between God's Word and the psalmist's hope, indicating that it is the promises of God that have sustained him through difficult times. This verse challenges us to reflect on our own sources of hope. Do we, like the psalmist, find our hope in the promises of God's Word, trusting that they will sustain us through trials, or do we look to temporary or worldly solutions that ultimately fail to provide lasting comfort?

In verse 50, the psalmist acknowledges the comfort he finds in God's promises: "This is my comfort in my affliction: for thy word hath quickened me." Here, the psalmist openly declares that it is God's Word that has given him life and vitality during times of affliction. The word "quickened" suggests a revival or renewal, as if the psalmist's spirit has been lifted and strengthened by the promises of Scripture. This verse underscores the transformative power of God's Word, especially when one is faced with suffering or hardship. The psalmist's experience challenges us to consider where we turn for comfort in our own afflictions. Do we, like the psalmist, rely on the life-giving power of God's Word to revive and strengthen us, or do we seek solace in other places that may not provide the deep, lasting comfort that Scripture offers?

The psalmist's determination to remain faithful despite opposition is evident in verse 51: "The proud have had me greatly in derision: yet have I not declined from thy law." This verse highlights the psalmist's steadfastness in the face of mockery and scorn from those who are proud and arrogant. The phrase "greatly in derision" suggests that the psalmist has been subjected to significant ridicule, yet he remains resolute in his commitment to God's law. The psalmist's unwavering adherence to God's commandments, even when faced with derision, is a powerful testament to his determination to live according to God's will, regardless of external pressures. This verse challenges us to reflect on how we respond to criticism or mockery for our faith. Do we, like the psalmist, remain firm in our commitment to God's law, or do we allow the opinions and judgments of others to sway us from the path of righteousness?

In verse 52, the psalmist finds strength in recalling God's past judgments: "I remembered thy judgments of old, O Lord; and have comforted myself." This verse reveals the psalmist's practice of reflecting on the history of God's righteous judgments as a source of comfort and reassurance. The phrase "thy judgments of old" suggests that the psalmist draws on the long history of God's faithfulness and justice, which provides him with the strength to endure present trials. By recalling how God has acted in the past, the psalmist is able to find solace and encouragement in the knowledge that God's character and promises are unchanging. This verse challenges us to consider how we use the past to inform our present faith. Do we, like the psalmist, remember and find comfort in the ways God has been faithful in the past, allowing those memories to strengthen our resolve in the face of current challenges, or do we forget or overlook the importance of reflecting on God's past works?

The psalmist's reaction to the wickedness around him is captured in verse 53: "Horror hath taken hold upon me because of the wicked that forsake thy law." This verse reflects the psalmist's deep distress and righteous anger at those who abandon God's law. The word "horror" conveys a sense of profound shock and dismay, as the psalmist grapples with the reality of wickedness and rebellion against God's commandments. The psalmist's reaction highlights his deep commitment to God's law and his sorrow over those who choose to forsake it. This verse challenges us to examine our own responses to the wickedness we observe in the world. Do we, like the psalmist, feel a deep sense of sorrow and horror when we see God's law being forsaken, or have we become desensitized or indifferent to the disobedience and sin around us?

In verse 54, the psalmist expresses how God's statutes have become a source of joy and comfort, even in the midst of his struggles: "Thy statutes have been my songs in the house of my pilgrimage." This verse reveals the psalmist's ability to find joy and solace in God's commandments, likening them to songs that uplift and sustain him during his journey through life. The phrase "house of my pilgrimage" suggests that the psalmist views his life as a temporary journey, with God's Word serving as a constant source of guidance and encouragement along the way. This verse challenges us to consider how we view and engage with God's commandments. Do we, like the psalmist, find joy in God's statutes, allowing them to be the songs that uplift and guide us through life's journey, or do we sometimes neglect or overlook the beauty and comfort that can be found in living according to God's Word?

The psalmist's commitment to remembering God's name and law is further emphasized in verse 55: "I have remembered thy name, O Lord, in the night, and have kept thy law." This verse highlights the psalmist's dedication to meditating on God's name and law, even during the night, a time often associated with rest or darkness. The phrase "in the night" suggests that the psalmist's devotion to God is not limited to the daylight hours but extends into the quiet, private moments when he reflects on God's character and commandments. The psalmist's practice of keeping God's law is presented as a natural outcome of his constant meditation on God's name. This verse challenges us to consider how we incorporate meditation on God's Word into our daily lives. Do we, like the psalmist, remember God's name and law even in the night, making it a habit to reflect on His character and commandments at all times, or do we confine our thoughts of God to specific moments, missing opportunities to deepen our relationship with Him?

The passage concludes in verse 56 with a declaration of the psalmist's steadfast commitment to obeying God's precepts: "This I had, because I kept thy precepts." This final verse encapsulates the psalmist's determination to hold onto God's Word as the foundation of his life. The phrase "this I had" suggests that the psalmist attributes the strength, comfort, and resilience he has experienced to his unwavering commitment to keeping God's precepts. By remaining faithful to God's commandments, the psalmist has been able to navigate the challenges and trials of life with a sense of purpose and direction. This verse challenges us to reflect on the role of God's precepts in our own lives. Do we, like the psalmist, recognize that the strength and comfort we experience in life are a result of our commitment to keeping God's precepts, or do we sometimes take for granted the benefits of living according to God's Word, failing to fully appreciate the blessings that come from obedience?

As we explore the theme of determination in Psalm 119, verses 49-56, we are reminded of the importance of holding onto God's promises and laws, even in the face of suffering, derision, and opposition. The psalmist's example challenges us to consider how we approach our relationship with God's Word, especially when confronted with trials and challenges. Do we, like the psalmist, remain determined to cling to God's promises, finding comfort and strength in His Word, or do we allow the difficulties of life to weaken our resolve and lead us away from the path of righteousness?

Furthermore, the psalmist's practice of recalling God's past judgments, his distress over the wickedness of those who forsake God's law, and his commitment to meditating on God's name and law challenge us to examine the depth of our own determination to live according to God's Word. Are we willing to draw strength from the history of God's faithfulness, to grieve over the disobedience we see in the world, and to make God's Word a constant presence in our lives, or do we sometimes falter in our commitment, allowing the pressures of life to distract us from our devotion to God?

In conclusion, the theme of determination in Psalm 119, verses 49-56, offers a powerful reminder of the need to anchor our lives in the promises and precepts of God's Word, especially when facing the challenges and adversities of life. The psalmist's unwavering resolve to hold onto God's Word, his commitment to living according to God's commandments, and his deep sense of sorrow over the forsaking of

God's law challenge us to deepen our own determination to live according to the truth of Scripture. As we continue to explore the depths of Psalm 119, may we be inspired to strengthen our resolve to hold onto God's promises, recognizing that it is through our determination to live according to His Word that we find the strength, comfort, and guidance we need to navigate the challenges and joys of life.

Whether we are facing criticism, seeking to grow in our understanding of God's Word, or striving to live a life that honors God, may we always turn to His Word as our source of determination and strength, knowing that it is through our commitment to His commandments that we find the true purpose and direction we need to live a life that is fully devoted to Him. The psalmist's example reminds us that true strength and resilience come not from our own efforts or from the world around us, but from the life-giving power of God's Word. By placing our trust in God's Word and seeking His guidance in every aspect of our lives, we can experience the peace, strength, and fulfillment that come from living a life that is anchored in the truth of His commandments. As we continue to journey through Psalm 119, may we be encouraged to deepen our determination to hold onto God's promises and laws, finding in them the wisdom, guidance, and strength we need to live a life that is fully devoted to Him, anchored in the truth of God's eternal Word.

Chapter 8 – The Discipline

In Psalm 119, verses 57-64, the theme of discipline is intricately woven as the psalmist reflects on the importance of self-discipline in keeping God's precepts, seeking His favor, and turning away from sin. These verses underscore the essential role of disciplined living in the life of a believer, illustrating how a commitment to God's Word requires consistent effort, intentionality, and a conscious decision to align one's life with divine principles. The psalmist begins in verse 57 with a powerful declaration: "Thou art my portion, O Lord: I have said that I would keep thy words." This opening statement reveals the psalmist's deep conviction that the Lord Himself is his inheritance, his most valuable possession. The phrase "Thou art my portion" signifies that the psalmist finds his ultimate satisfaction and fulfillment in God alone, rather than in material wealth or worldly achievements. By declaring his intention to "keep thy words," the psalmist expresses a resolute commitment to live according to God's commandments, recognizing that this requires disciplined adherence to the precepts of Scripture. This verse challenges us to consider where we place our true value and commitment. Do we, like the psalmist, view God as our portion, dedicating ourselves to keeping His Word with unwavering discipline, or do we sometimes allow other pursuits to take precedence, neglecting the disciplined life that God calls us to?

In verse 58, the psalmist continues with a heartfelt plea for God's favor: "I intreated thy favour with my whole heart: be merciful unto me according to thy word." This verse highlights the psalmist's earnest desire to seek God's favor, not half-heartedly, but with his entire being. The phrase "with my whole heart" emphasizes the depth of the psalmist's devotion and the intensity of his plea, indicating that his pursuit of God's favor is not casual or superficial but is driven by a deep, sincere longing for God's presence and blessing. The request for mercy "according to thy word" underscores the psalmist's reliance on

God's promises as the foundation for his plea, reflecting his disciplined focus on Scripture as the source of divine grace and guidance. This verse challenges us to examine the sincerity and intensity of our own pursuit of God's favor. Are we, like the psalmist, seeking God with our whole heart, disciplined in our devotion and reliance on His Word, or do we sometimes approach our relationship with God with less than full commitment, lacking the depth and consistency that true discipline requires?

The psalmist's commitment to self-examination and repentance is evident in verse 59: "I thought on my ways, and turned my feet unto thy testimonies." This verse reveals the psalmist's practice of regular self-reflection, a key aspect of disciplined living. The phrase "I thought on my ways" indicates that the psalmist takes time to carefully consider his actions, attitudes, and the direction of his life. This introspection leads him to "turn my feet unto thy testimonies," signifying a deliberate decision to correct his course and align his life with God's commandments. This verse challenges us to reflect on how we approach self-examination and repentance in our own lives. Do we, like the psalmist, regularly assess our ways and make the necessary adjustments to stay aligned with God's Word, or do we neglect this vital practice, allowing ourselves to drift away from the disciplined life that God desires for us?

In verse 60, the psalmist emphasizes the urgency and immediacy of his obedience: "I made haste, and delayed not to keep thy commandments." This verse highlights the psalmist's sense of urgency in obeying God's Word, demonstrating that he does not procrastinate or hesitate when it comes to following God's commands. The phrases "made haste" and "delayed not" suggest that the psalmist understands the importance of prompt and decisive action in living a disciplined life. He recognizes that delaying obedience can lead to missed opportunities, increased temptation, and a weakening of one's resolve. This verse challenges us to consider how we respond to God's commands in our own lives. Do we, like the psalmist, act with urgency and determination to keep God's commandments, or do we sometimes delay or hesitate, allowing distractions or doubts to hinder our obedience and disrupt our disciplined walk with God?

The psalmist's perseverance in the face of opposition is highlighted in verse 61: "The bands of the wicked have robbed me: but I have not forgotten thy law." This verse reveals that despite the hardships and injustices inflicted upon him by the wicked, the psalmist remains steadfast in his commitment to God's law. The phrase "the bands of the wicked have robbed me" suggests that the psalmist has suffered significant loss at the hands of those who oppose him, yet he does not allow this to deter him from following God's commandments. His unwavering focus on God's law, even in the midst of adversity, is a testament to his disciplined faith and determination. This verse challenges us to consider how we respond to difficulties and opposition in our own lives. Do we, like the psalmist, remain committed to God's law even when faced with hardship and loss, or do we allow external circumstances to shake our resolve and lead us away from the disciplined life that God calls us to?

In verse 62, the psalmist expresses his disciplined practice of worship and gratitude: "At midnight I will rise to give thanks unto thee because of thy righteous judgments." This verse highlights the psalmist's commitment to offering thanks to God, even during the quiet, solitary hours of the night. The phrase "at midnight I will rise" indicates that the psalmist's discipline extends to his worship practices, as he makes a deliberate effort to praise God for His righteous judgments, regardless of the time or his personal circumstances. This verse challenges us to examine the consistency and intentionality of our own worship and expressions of gratitude. Are we, like the psalmist, disciplined in our practice of giving thanks to God, even when it requires sacrifice or effort, or do we sometimes neglect this important aspect of our spiritual lives, allowing other priorities to take precedence?

The psalmist's commitment to fellowship with others who fear God is evident in verse 63: "I am a companion of all them that fear thee, and of them that keep thy precepts." This verse underscores the importance of surrounding oneself with like-minded individuals who share a reverence for God and a commitment to His precepts. The phrase "I am a companion" suggests that the psalmist deliberately chooses to associate with those who are also devoted to living according to God's commandments, recognizing that such relationships can provide support, encouragement, and accountability in maintaining a disciplined life. This verse challenges us to reflect on the company we keep and the influence it has on our spiritual discipline. Do we, like the psalmist, seek out and build relationships with those who fear God and keep His precepts, recognizing the value of such companionship in our own walk with God, or do we allow ourselves to be influenced by those who may lead us away from the disciplined life that God desires for us?

The passage concludes in verse 64 with a recognition of God's unfailing love and a plea for further instruction: "The earth, O Lord, is full of thy mercy: teach me thy statutes." This final verse encapsulates the psalmist's acknowledgment of God's abundant mercy, which is evident throughout all creation. The phrase "the earth is full of thy mercy" reflects the psalmist's deep awareness of God's lovingkindness and the many ways it is manifested in the world around him. Despite his awareness of God's mercy, the psalmist remains committed to learning and living by God's statutes, as indicated by his plea, "teach me thy statutes." This verse challenges us to consider how we respond to the recognition of God's mercy in our own lives. Do we, like the psalmist, allow our awareness of God's unfailing love to drive us to a deeper commitment to learning and obeying His Word, or do we take God's mercy for granted, failing to respond with the disciplined obedience that such love calls for?

As we explore the theme of discipline in Psalm 119, verses 57-64, we are reminded of the crucial role that self-discipline plays in living a life that is fully devoted to God's Word. The psalmist's example challenges us to consider how we approach our relationship with God's commandments, especially in terms of our commitment to consistent, intentional obedience. Do we, like the psalmist, view God as our portion and dedicate ourselves to keeping His Word with unwavering discipline, or do we sometimes allow other pursuits and distractions to interfere with our commitment to living according to God's precepts?

Furthermore, the psalmist's emphasis on self-examination, prompt obedience, perseverance in the face of opposition, disciplined worship, and the importance of godly companionship challenges us to examine the various aspects of our own spiritual discipline. Are we regularly assessing our ways and making the necessary adjustments to stay aligned with God's Word? Do we act with urgency and determination to keep God's commandments, even when faced with difficulties or opposition? Are we consistent in our practice of worship and gratitude, and do we seek out relationships with those who share our commitment to living according to God's precepts?

In conclusion, the theme of discipline in Psalm 119, verses 57-64, offers a powerful reminder of the importance of living a life that is fully anchored in the truth of God's Word, marked by intentionality, consistency, and a deep commitment to following God's commandments. The psalmist's unwavering resolve to live according to God's precepts, his practice of self-examination and repentance, and his disciplined approach to worship and fellowship challenge us to deepen our own commitment to a disciplined life that honors God. As we continue to explore the

depths of Psalm 119, may we be inspired to strengthen our self-discipline in keeping God's commandments, seeking His favor, and turning away from sin, recognizing that it is through such discipline that we find the true freedom, joy, and fulfillment that come from living a life that is fully devoted to Him.

Whether we are striving to grow in our understanding of God's Word, seeking to live a life that honors God, or facing the challenges and distractions of the world, may we always turn to His Word as our guide and anchor, knowing that it is through disciplined obedience to His commandments that we find the strength, wisdom, and peace we need to navigate the complexities and joys of life. The psalmist's example reminds us that true discipline is not a matter of rigid adherence to rules, but a deeply rooted commitment to living according to the truth of God's Word, driven by a sincere desire to honor and please the Lord in all that we do. By placing our trust in God's Word and seeking His guidance in every aspect of our lives, we can experience the fullness of life that comes from living a disciplined life that is anchored in the truth of His eternal Word. As we continue to journey through Psalm 119, may we be encouraged to deepen our commitment to self-discipline, finding in God's Word the strength, guidance, and inspiration we need to live a life that is fully devoted to Him, anchored in the truth of God's eternal Word.

Chapter 9 – The Deliverance

In Psalm 119, verses 65-72, the theme of deliverance is powerfully explored as the psalmist reflects on the way God's Word brings rescue and salvation while also imparting valuable lessons through trials and afflictions. These verses provide a deep, heartfelt testimony to the psalmist's understanding that life's difficulties are not meaningless but are used by God to shape, teach, and ultimately deliver those who trust in Him. The psalmist begins in verse 65 with a statement of faith in God's goodness: "Thou hast dealt well with thy servant, O Lord, according unto thy word." This opening declaration sets the tone for the entire passage, as the psalmist acknowledges that God has treated him with kindness and faithfulness, just as promised in Scripture. The phrase "according unto thy word" emphasizes the psalmist's trust in God's Word as the ultimate standard of truth and goodness, underscoring that God's actions are always in alignment with His promises. This verse challenges us to consider our own recognition of God's goodness in our lives, especially in the face of adversity. Do we, like the psalmist, see God's hand at work, dealing well with us according to His Word, even when our circumstances are difficult, or do we sometimes lose sight of God's faithfulness when trials arise?

In verse 66, the psalmist expresses a desire for greater wisdom and discernment: "Teach me good judgment and knowledge: for I have believed thy commandments." Here, the psalmist recognizes that true wisdom comes from God and is found in understanding and applying His commandments. The request for "good judgment and knowledge" indicates a longing for the ability to make wise decisions based on a deep understanding of God's Word. The psalmist's belief in God's commandments is the foundation for this request, showing that he trusts in the reliability and truth of Scripture as the source of all wisdom. This verse challenges us to examine our own pursuit of wisdom. Do we, like the psalmist, seek God's guidance for good judgment and knowledge, believing that His commandments are the ultimate source of truth, or do we rely on our own understanding or the shifting wisdom of the world?

The psalmist's acknowledgment of the value of affliction is expressed in verse 67: "Before I was afflicted I went astray: but now have I kept thy word." This verse reveals a profound truth about the role of suffering in spiritual growth. The psalmist admits that before experiencing affliction, he had wandered away from God's path, but the difficulties he faced led him back to obedience. The phrase "but now have I kept thy word" indicates that the trials the psalmist endured served as a corrective measure, bringing him closer to God and His commandments. This verse challenges us to reflect on how we view our own afflictions. Do we, like the psalmist, recognize that God can use our trials to draw us back to Him and to teach us the importance of obedience, or do we resist and resent the difficulties we face, failing to see the potential for growth and deliverance that they offer?

In verse 68, the psalmist reaffirms God's goodness and asks for continued instruction: "Thou art good, and doest good; teach me thy statutes." This verse underscores the psalmist's unwavering belief in the goodness of God, even in the midst of trials. The phrase "thou art good, and doest good" is a powerful declaration of faith, acknowledging that God's nature and actions are inherently good, regardless of the circumstances. The psalmist's request for God to "teach me thy statutes" reflects a desire to continue learning and growing in understanding, recognizing that God's laws are a reflection of His goodness and a guide to living a righteous life. This verse challenges us to consider our own attitude toward God's character and commandments. Do we, like the psalmist, trust in God's goodness and seek to learn more about His statutes, even when we are going through difficult times, or do we question God's goodness and withdraw from His Word when life becomes challenging?

The psalmist's awareness of opposition and slander is evident in verse 69: "The proud have forged a lie against me: but I will keep thy precepts with my whole heart." This verse reveals the psalmist's experience of being falsely accused and slandered by those who are proud and arrogant. Despite the lies and opposition he faces, the psalmist remains committed to keeping God's precepts with all his heart. The phrase "with my whole heart" indicates a total, undivided commitment to living according to God's commandments, even in the face of adversity and falsehood. This verse challenges us to reflect on how we respond to opposition and slander in our own lives. Do we, like the psalmist, remain steadfast in our commitment to God's precepts, even when others lie about us or seek to harm us, or do we allow the attacks of others to shake our faith and lead us away from God's truth?

In verse 70, the psalmist contrasts the hard-heartedness of the wicked with his own delight in God's law: "Their heart is as fat as grease; but I delight in thy law." This verse highlights the difference between those who are spiritually insensitive and self-indulgent, represented by the phrase "their heart is as fat as grease," and the psalmist, who finds joy and satisfaction in God's law. The psalmist's delight in God's law stands in stark contrast to the spiritual dullness of those who reject God's commandments, showing that true fulfillment comes from living in accordance with God's Word. This verse challenges us to examine the condition of our own hearts. Do we, like the psalmist, find delight in God's law, allowing it to bring us joy and fulfillment, or have we allowed our hearts to become hardened and indifferent to the truth of Scripture?

The psalmist's recognition of the benefits of affliction is further emphasized in verse 71: "It is good for me that I have been afflicted; that I might learn thy statutes." This verse reveals the psalmist's understanding that affliction, though painful, has brought about a positive outcome by leading him to a deeper understanding of God's statutes. The phrase "it is good for me" suggests that the psalmist has come to appreciate the value of his trials, recognizing that they have served as a catalyst for spiritual growth and greater obedience. This verse challenges us to consider how we view the difficulties we face in life. Do we, like the psalmist, see our afflictions as opportunities to learn and grow in our understanding of God's Word, or do we view them as obstacles to be avoided or resented, missing the valuable lessons they can teach us?

The passage concludes in verse 72 with a declaration of the incomparable value of God's law: "The law of thy mouth is better unto me than thousands of gold and silver." This final verse encapsulates the psalmist's deep appreciation for God's Word, valuing it more highly than material wealth. The phrase "better unto me than thousands of gold and silver" reflects the psalmist's recognition that the wisdom, guidance, and deliverance found in God's law are far more valuable than any earthly riches. This verse challenges us to examine our own priorities and values. Do we, like the psalmist, place the highest value on God's law, recognizing it as our most precious possession, or do we sometimes prioritize material wealth and worldly success over the spiritual riches that come from living according to God's Word?

As we explore the theme of deliverance in Psalm 119, verses 65-72, we are reminded of the profound truth that God's Word brings both rescue and teaching through the trials we face in life. The psalmist's example challenges us to consider how we approach our relationship with God's Word, especially in times of difficulty and affliction. Do we, like the psalmist, trust in God's goodness and recognize that our trials can serve as valuable lessons that draw us closer to Him and deepen our understanding of His statutes, or do we resist and resent the challenges we face, failing to see the potential for growth and deliverance that they offer?

Furthermore, the psalmist's recognition of the value of affliction, his commitment to keeping God's precepts with his whole heart, and his deep appreciation for the incomparable worth of God's law challenge us to examine the depth of our own commitment to living according to God's Word. Are we willing to embrace the trials we face as opportunities for spiritual growth and deeper obedience? Do we remain steadfast in our commitment to God's precepts, even in the face of opposition and slander? And do we truly value God's law as our most precious possession, recognizing that it is through His Word that we find true deliverance, wisdom, and fulfillment?

In conclusion, the theme of deliverance in Psalm 119, verses 65-72, offers a powerful reminder of the need to anchor our lives in the truth and wisdom of God's Word, especially when facing the challenges and trials of life. The psalmist's deep trust in God's goodness, his understanding of the value of affliction, and his unwavering commitment to keeping God's precepts with his whole heart challenge us to deepen our own reliance on God's Word as the source of our deliverance and guidance. As we continue to explore the depths of Psalm 119, may we be inspired to recognize the valuable lessons that our trials can teach us, and to remain steadfast in our commitment to living according to God's Word, knowing that it is through His commandments that we find the true deliverance, wisdom, and fulfillment we need to navigate the complexities and joys of life.

Whether we are facing opposition, seeking to grow in our understanding of God's Word, or striving to live a life that honors God, may we always turn to His Word as our source of deliverance and guidance, knowing that it is through our commitment to His commandments that we find the true purpose and direction we need to live a life that is fully devoted to Him. The psalmist's example reminds us that true deliverance and wisdom come not from avoiding or resenting the trials we face, but from embracing them as opportunities for growth and deeper obedience to God's Word. By placing our trust in God's Word and seeking His guidance in every aspect of our lives, we can experience the peace, strength, and fulfillment that come from living a life that is anchored in the truth of His commandments. As we continue to journey through Psalm 119, may we be encouraged to deepen our commitment to seeking deliverance and wisdom through God's Word, finding in it the strength, guidance, and inspiration we need to live a life that is fully devoted to Him, anchored in the truth of God's eternal Word.

Chapter 10 – The Devotion

In Psalm 119, verses 73-80, the theme of devotion is deeply explored as the psalmist reaffirms his unwavering commitment to God's commandments, while also seeking wisdom and compassion from the Lord. These verses reveal the psalmist's profound understanding of his relationship with God, acknowledging both the responsibility and the privilege of being guided by God's Word. The passage begins in verse 73 with a declaration of God's creative power and a plea for understanding: "Thy hands have made me and fashioned me: give me understanding, that I may learn thy commandments." This opening verse reflects the psalmist's recognition that, as a creation of God, he is intricately designed and purposefully made. The acknowledgment that "thy hands have made me and fashioned me" underscores the intimate connection between the Creator and the created, highlighting the psalmist's dependence on God for life and guidance. The psalmist's request for understanding, "that I may learn thy commandments," emphasizes his deep desire to align his life with God's will, recognizing that true wisdom comes from understanding and following the divine laws set forth in Scripture. This verse challenges us to consider our own sense of devotion to God's commandments. Do we, like the psalmist, recognize that our lives are purposefully designed by God and seek understanding to live in accordance with His Word, or do we sometimes neglect the importance of learning and applying God's commandments in our daily lives?

In verse 74, the psalmist expresses his hope that others who fear God will find encouragement in his faithfulness: "They that fear thee will be glad when they see me; because I have hoped in thy word." This verse highlights the psalmist's awareness of the influence his devotion to God's Word can have on others. The phrase "they that fear thee" refers to those who revere and honor God, and the psalmist's hope is that his steadfastness in hoping in God's Word will bring joy and encouragement to fellow believers. This verse challenges us to reflect on the impact of our own devotion to God's Word on those around us. Do we, like the psalmist, strive to be an example of faithfulness that brings encouragement and gladness to others who share our reverence for God, or do we sometimes fail to recognize the influence our devotion can have on the community of believers?

The psalmist's acknowledgment of God's righteous judgments and a plea for comfort in affliction is evident in verse 75: "I know, O Lord, that thy judgments are right, and that thou in faithfulness hast afflicted me." This verse reveals the psalmist's deep trust in the righteousness of God's decisions, even when they involve personal suffering. The phrase "thy judgments are right" reflects the psalmist's conviction that God's ways are just and true, and the acknowledgment that "thou in faithfulness hast afflicted me" demonstrates the psalmist's understanding that affliction can be an expression of God's faithfulness—a means of correction and refinement. This verse challenges us to consider how we respond to the trials and difficulties we face. Do we, like the psalmist, trust in the righteousness of God's judgments and recognize that even our afflictions can be a sign of His faithfulness, or do we struggle to see the purpose and goodness in our suffering, questioning God's justice and care?

In verse 76, the psalmist seeks God's mercy as a source of comfort: "Let, I pray thee, thy merciful kindness be for my comfort, according to thy word unto thy servant." This verse highlights the psalmist's deep desire for the comfort that comes from experiencing God's mercy. The phrase "thy merciful kindness" refers to God's steadfast love and compassion, which the psalmist longs to feel in the midst of his afflictions. By asking for comfort "according to thy word," the psalmist reaffirms his trust in the promises of Scripture, recognizing that God's Word is the foundation for experiencing His mercy and kindness. This verse challenges us to reflect on where we seek comfort in times of distress. Do we, like the psalmist, turn to God's merciful kindness and the promises of His Word as our primary source of comfort, or do we sometimes look for solace in temporary or worldly solutions that ultimately fail to provide lasting peace?

The psalmist's plea for compassion and protection from the arrogance of others is expressed in verse 77: "Let thy tender mercies come unto me, that I may live: for thy law is my delight." This verse reveals the psalmist's dependence on God's compassion as the source of life and vitality. The phrase "thy tender mercies" reflects the psalmist's understanding of God's gentle, nurturing care, which he sees as essential for his survival and well-being. The psalmist's declaration that "thy law is my delight" underscores his deep love for God's commandments, viewing them not as a burden, but as a source of joy and fulfillment. This verse challenges us to examine our own attitude toward God's law and our reliance on His compassion. Do we, like the psalmist, delight in God's law and seek His tender mercies as the source of our life and well-being, or do we sometimes resist God's commandments and fail to recognize the life-giving power of His compassion?

In verse 78, the psalmist asks for deliverance from those who wrongfully oppose him: "Let the proud be ashamed; for they dealt perversely with me without a cause: but I will meditate in thy precepts." This verse highlights the psalmist's resolve to remain focused on God's Word, even in the face of unjust treatment by the proud and arrogant. The phrase "let the proud be ashamed" reflects the psalmist's desire for justice, that those who act wrongly against him will be brought to shame. However, rather than seeking personal revenge, the psalmist chooses to "meditate in thy precepts," showing his commitment to staying anchored in God's commandments, regardless of the actions of others. This verse challenges us to consider how we respond to unjust treatment and opposition. Do we, like the psalmist, remain committed to meditating on God's precepts and trusting in His justice, or do we sometimes become consumed by a desire for retribution, losing sight of the importance of staying grounded in God's Word?

The psalmist's expression of devotion through fellowship with others who fear God is evident in verse 79: "Let those that fear thee turn unto me, and those that have known thy testimonies." This verse reveals the psalmist's desire for companionship with others who share his reverence for God and his commitment to God's testimonies. The phrase "let those that fear thee turn unto me" reflects the psalmist's longing for a community of like-minded believers who can offer support, encouragement, and mutual devotion to God's Word. This verse challenges us to reflect on the importance of fellowship in our own spiritual journey. Do we, like the psalmist, seek out and value relationships with others who fear God and share our commitment to His testimonies, recognizing the strength and encouragement that comes from such fellowship, or do we sometimes neglect the importance of building and maintaining these vital connections within the body of believers?

The passage concludes in verse 80 with a prayer for integrity and protection from shame: "Let my heart be sound in thy statutes; that I be not ashamed." This final verse encapsulates the psalmist's desire for a heart that is fully aligned with God's statutes, free from any wavering or duplicity. The phrase "let my heart be sound" suggests a desire for wholeness and integrity, a heart that is steadfast and true in its devotion to God's commandments. The psalmist's concern "that I be not ashamed" reflects his understanding that living in accordance with God's Word is the key to avoiding the shame and disgrace that come from sin and disobedience. This verse challenges us to consider the condition of our own hearts and our commitment to living with integrity according to God's statutes. Do we, like the psalmist, desire a heart that is sound and steadfast in its devotion to God's commandments, recognizing that this is the path to living a life free from shame, or do we sometimes allow our hearts to be divided, compromising our integrity and risking the consequences of disobedience?

As we explore the theme of devotion in Psalm 119, verses 73-80, we are reminded of the importance of reaffirming our commitment to God's commandments and seeking His wisdom and compassion in every aspect of our lives. The psalmist's example challenges us to consider how we approach our relationship with God's Word, especially in terms of our devotion to learning, understanding, and applying His commandments. Do we, like the psalmist, recognize that our lives are purposefully designed by God and seek wisdom and understanding to live in accordance with His Word, or do we sometimes neglect the importance of deepening our devotion to God's commandments?

Furthermore, the psalmist's emphasis on the influence of his devotion on others, his trust in God's righteous judgments, his reliance on God's mercy and compassion, and his commitment to fellowship with those who fear God challenge us to examine the depth of our own devotion to living according to God's Word. Are we aware of the impact our devotion can have on others, and do we strive to be an example of faithfulness that brings encouragement to fellow believers? Do we trust in the righteousness of God's judgments, even in times of affliction, and seek His mercy as our primary source of comfort and strength? And do we value and seek out fellowship with other believers who share our reverence for God, recognizing the importance of building a strong community of faith?

In conclusion, the theme of devotion in Psalm 119, verses 73-80, offers a powerful reminder of the need to anchor

our lives in a deep and abiding commitment to God's commandments, while also seeking His wisdom and compassion to guide us through the challenges and joys of life. The psalmist's unwavering devotion to God's Word, his reliance on God's mercy and compassion, and his commitment to fellowship with other believers challenge us to deepen our own devotion to living according to God's commandments. As we continue to explore the depths of Psalm 119, may we be inspired to reaffirm our commitment to God's Word, seeking His wisdom and compassion in every aspect of our lives, and recognizing that it is through our devotion to His commandments that we find true strength, guidance, and fulfillment.

Whether we are seeking to grow in our understanding of God's Word, striving to live a life that honors God, or facing the challenges and temptations of the world, may we always turn to His Word as our source of guidance and inspiration, knowing that it is through our devotion to His commandments that we find the true purpose and direction we need to live a life that is fully devoted to Him. The psalmist's example reminds us that true devotion is not just about outward actions, but about the condition of our hearts and our commitment to living according to the truth of God's Word. By placing our trust in God's Word and seeking His wisdom and compassion in every aspect of our lives, we can experience the fullness of life that comes from living a life that is anchored in the truth of His eternal Word. As we continue to journey through Psalm 119, may we be encouraged to deepen our devotion to God's commandments, finding in His Word the strength, guidance, and inspiration we need to live a life that is fully devoted to Him, anchored in the truth of God's eternal Word.

Chapter 11 – The Desperation

In Psalm 119, verses 81-88, the theme of desperation is poignantly and powerfully explored as the psalmist expresses an intense longing for salvation and clings desperately to hope in God's promises amid severe trials. These verses offer a raw, unfiltered glimpse into the soul of someone who is enduring deep affliction, yet who remains anchored in the unshakeable truth of God's Word. The psalmist begins in verse 81 with a cry from the depths of his soul: "My soul fainteth for thy salvation: but I hope in thy word." This opening verse captures the essence of desperation, as the psalmist reveals that his soul is nearly overwhelmed, on the verge of collapse under the weight of his afflictions. The phrase "fainteth for thy salvation" suggests a yearning so intense that it has brought him to the point of physical and emotional exhaustion. Yet, even in this weakened state, the psalmist does not give up; instead, he clings to hope in God's Word. The word "but" in this verse is crucial, indicating that despite the psalmist's desperate condition, his hope is undiminished because it is rooted in the promises of Scripture. This verse challenges us to reflect on how we respond in our own moments of desperation. Do we, like the psalmist, cling to hope in God's Word even when our circumstances are overwhelming, or do we allow despair to overshadow our trust in God's promises?

In verse 82, the psalmist continues to express his deep longing for God's intervention: "Mine eyes fail for thy word, saying, When wilt thou comfort me?" This verse builds on the theme of desperation, with the psalmist describing how his eyes are weary from searching for the fulfillment of God's promises. The phrase "mine eyes fail" conveys the idea that the psalmist has been looking expectantly for God's deliverance for so long that he has become physically and emotionally drained. The question "When wilt thou comfort me?" reveals the psalmist's deep need for reassurance, as he longs for the comfort that only God can provide. This verse challenges us to consider our own patience and persistence in waiting for God's promises to be fulfilled. Do we, like the psalmist, continue to look to God's Word for comfort and assurance, even when it seems like our prayers are going unanswered, or do we become discouraged and give up on seeking God's intervention?

The psalmist's sense of being worn down by his trials is further emphasized in verse 83: "For I am become like a bottle in the smoke; yet do I not forget thy statutes." This vivid metaphor compares the psalmist's condition to that of a wineskin, or bottle, shriveled and blackened by exposure to smoke. The image of a bottle in the smoke suggests a state of neglect, weariness, and decay, yet the psalmist's commitment to God's Word remains firm. The phrase "yet do I not forget thy statutes" reveals that despite his suffering, the psalmist refuses to let go of his devotion to God's commandments. This verse challenges us to reflect on our own faithfulness in the face of hardship. Do we, like the psalmist, remain committed to God's Word even when our circumstances leave us feeling worn out and abandoned, or do we allow our difficulties to weaken our resolve and lead us away from the truths that sustain us?

In verse 84, the psalmist voices a poignant question that reflects his growing desperation: "How many are the days of thy servant? When wilt thou execute judgment on them that persecute me?" This verse reveals the psalmist's awareness of the brevity of life and the urgency of his situation. The question "How many are the days of thy servant?" suggests that the psalmist is acutely aware that his time on earth is limited, and he longs for God to intervene before it is too late. The plea for God to "execute judgment" on those who persecute him indicates the psalmist's deep desire for justice and deliverance from his oppressors. This verse challenges us to consider how we handle feelings of injustice and the desire for God's intervention. Do we, like the psalmist, cry out to God for justice, trusting in His timing, or do we become impatient or bitter when it seems like God is slow to act on our behalf?

The psalmist's awareness of the relentless nature of his enemies is highlighted in verse 85: "The proud have digged pits for me, which are not after thy law." This verse describes the malicious intent of those who oppose the psalmist, likening their actions to the digging of pits—traps meant to ensnare and harm him. The phrase "which are not after thy law" indicates that the psalmist's enemies are acting in direct violation of God's commandments, further underscoring the injustice of their actions. Despite the constant threat posed by his enemies, the psalmist remains focused on God's law, recognizing that his adversaries' actions are not only against him but against God's righteous standards. This verse challenges us to reflect on how we respond to the actions of those who oppose us. Do we, like the psalmist, remain steadfast in our commitment to God's law, even when faced with the malice and deceit of others, or do we allow the actions of our enemies to shake our faith and lead us away from God's truth?

In verse 86, the psalmist declares his trust in the truth of God's commandments while pleading for divine help: "All thy commandments are faithful: they persecute me wrongfully; help thou me." This verse reveals the psalmist's deep conviction that God's commandments are entirely trustworthy and faithful. Despite the wrongful persecution he is enduring, the psalmist does not waver in his belief that God's Word is true and reliable. The urgent plea "help thou me" reflects the psalmist's desperation for divine assistance, as he recognizes that only God can deliver him from his persecutors. This verse challenges us to consider the strength of our own trust in God's Word. Do we, like the psalmist, maintain our trust in the faithfulness of God's commandments, even when we are unjustly persecuted or face difficult circumstances, or do we allow doubt to creep in and weaken our faith?

The psalmist's sense of near-despair is expressed in verse 87: "They had almost consumed me upon earth; but I forsook not thy precepts." This verse vividly conveys the intensity of the psalmist's trials, as he describes how his enemies have nearly succeeded in destroying him. The phrase "almost consumed me upon earth" suggests that the psalmist has been pushed to the brink of ruin, yet even in this dire situation, he remains committed to God's precepts. The determination to "forsake not thy precepts" highlights the psalmist's unwavering devotion to God's Word, even in the face of overwhelming adversity. This verse challenges us to reflect on our own perseverance in the face of extreme difficulties. Do we, like the psalmist, refuse to forsake God's precepts, even when it feels like we are on the verge of being consumed by our trials, or do we give in to despair and abandon the principles that have guided us?

The passage concludes in verse 88 with a prayer for revival and continued obedience: "Quicken me after thy lovingkindness; so shall I keep the testimony of thy mouth." This final verse encapsulates the psalmist's deep desire for spiritual renewal and his commitment to continued obedience to God's Word. The phrase "quicken me after thy lovingkindness" reflects the psalmist's recognition that true life and vitality come from God's loving and gracious intervention. By asking God to quicken him, the psalmist is seeking a revival of spirit that will enable him to continue living in accordance with God's commandments. The commitment to "keep the testimony of thy mouth" underscores the psalmist's determination to remain faithful to God's Word, no matter the circumstances. This verse challenges us to consider our own need for spiritual renewal and our commitment to obedience. Do we, like the psalmist, seek God's lovingkindness to quicken and revive our spirits, so that we can continue to live in accordance with His Word, or do we sometimes neglect the need for renewal and allow our spiritual fervor to wane?

As we explore the theme of desperation in Psalm 119, verses 81-88, we are reminded of the profound importance of clinging to hope in God's promises, even in the most challenging and desperate circumstances. The psalmist's example challenges us to consider how we respond to the trials and afflictions we face in our own lives. Do we, like the psalmist, remain anchored in the truth of God's Word, trusting in His promises even when our souls are faint and our eyes fail from searching for deliverance, or do we allow despair and hopelessness to take root, leading us away from the comfort and assurance that Scripture provides?

Furthermore, the psalmist's unwavering commitment to God's precepts, even in the face of severe persecution and near-despair, challenges us to examine the depth of our own devotion to living according to God's Word. Are we willing to hold fast to God's commandments, trusting in His justice and faithfulness, even when we are wrongfully persecuted or face overwhelming opposition? Do we seek God's help and rely on His lovingkindness to revive and sustain us, recognizing that our true strength and hope come from Him alone?

In conclusion, the theme of desperation in Psalm 119, verses 81-88, offers a powerful reminder of the need to anchor our lives in the truth and promises of God's Word, especially in times of intense trial and affliction.

The psalmist's raw and honest expression of desperation, combined with his unwavering hope in God's Word and his commitment to continued obedience, challenges us to deepen our own reliance on Scripture as our source of comfort, strength, and guidance. As we continue to explore the depths of Psalm 119, may we be inspired to cling to God's promises with unwavering hope, even in our most desperate moments, recognizing that it is through our faith in His Word that we find the true deliverance, wisdom, and peace we need to navigate the complexities and challenges of life.

Whether we are facing severe trials, seeking to grow in our understanding of God's Word, or striving to live a life that honors God, may we always turn to His Word as our source of hope and salvation, knowing that it is through our commitment to His commandments that we find the true purpose and direction we need to live a life that is fully devoted to Him. The psalmist's example reminds us that true deliverance and hope are found not in our circumstances, but in the unchanging truth of God's Word. By placing our trust in God's promises and seeking His guidance in every aspect of our lives, we can experience the peace, strength, and fulfillment that come from living a life that is anchored in the truth of His commandments. As we continue to journey through Psalm 119, may we be encouraged to deepen our commitment to seeking deliverance and hope through God's Word, finding in it the strength, guidance, and inspiration we need to live a life that is fully devoted to Him, anchored in the truth of God's eternal Word.

Chapter 12 – The Discernment

In Psalm 119, verses 89-96, the theme of discernment is profoundly explored as the psalmist acknowledges the critical need for wisdom and understanding that comes from God's eternal Word, which stands firm in the heavens. These verses reflect the psalmist's deep recognition that true discernment—the ability to make wise, godly decisions—can only be rooted in the unchanging truth of God's commandments. The psalmist begins in verse 89 with a powerful declaration of the eternal nature of God's Word: "For ever, O Lord, thy word is settled in heaven." This opening verse establishes the foundation for the psalmist's understanding of discernment, emphasizing that God's Word is not just relevant for a moment in time, but is eternally established, unalterable, and reliable. The phrase "settled in heaven" conveys the idea that God's Word is fixed and secure, beyond the reach of human tampering or the shifting sands of cultural trends. This verse challenges us to consider the stability and permanence of God's Word in our own lives. Do we, like the psalmist, recognize that true discernment must be anchored in the eternal truth of Scripture, which remains steadfast regardless of the changing circumstances of our lives and the world around us, or do we sometimes rely on transient human wisdom or personal preferences to guide our decisions?

In verse 90, the psalmist continues to reflect on the faithfulness of God through generations: "Thy faithfulness is unto all generations: thou hast established the earth, and it abideth." This verse reinforces the idea that God's Word is not only eternal but also consistently reliable across all generations. The psalmist's acknowledgment that God "hast established the earth, and it abideth" serves as a reminder that just as the physical world is upheld by God's power, so too is His Word upheld by His unchanging nature. The reference to God's faithfulness spanning "unto all generations" underscores the enduring relevance of Scripture, offering a timeless guide for discernment that applies to every person, in every era. This verse challenges us to reflect on how we view the relevance of God's Word in our own lives. Do we, like the psalmist, see God's faithfulness as a guarantee that His Word will always be a reliable source of wisdom and guidance, or do we sometimes question whether Scripture is applicable to our modern-day challenges and decisions?

The psalmist's trust in God's sustaining power is further expressed in verse 91: "They continue this day according to thine ordinances: for all are thy servants." Here, the psalmist acknowledges that all of creation continues to exist and function according to God's divine ordinances, which are His established laws governing the universe. The phrase "for all are thy servants" highlights the idea that everything in creation operates under God's authority, fulfilling His purposes. This recognition of God's sovereign control over all things serves as a foundation for the psalmist's discernment, affirming that if the natural world is governed by God's laws, then human lives must also be guided by the wisdom of His Word. This verse challenges us to consider how we align our lives with God's ordinances. Do we, like the psalmist, recognize that just as creation is subject to God's laws, so too should our decisions and actions be governed by the discernment that comes from His Word, or do we sometimes act as though we are exempt from the divine principles that God has established?

In verse 92, the psalmist reveals the life-saving impact of God's Word during times of affliction: "Unless thy law had been my delights, I should then have perished in mine affliction." This verse powerfully conveys the idea that the psalmist's very survival depended on his love for and adherence to God's law. The phrase "my delights" indicates that the psalmist found great joy and satisfaction in God's commandments, which served as a source of strength and comfort during his times of suffering. The recognition that without this delight in God's law, he "should then have perished" underscores the life-sustaining power of Scripture, which not only provides discernment but also the resilience needed to endure hardships. This verse challenges us to reflect on where we find our strength in times of trouble. Do we, like the psalmist, delight in God's Word and rely on it as our source of discernment and survival during affliction, or do we seek solace in other, less dependable sources that cannot provide the same enduring support?

The psalmist's commitment to remembering and obeying God's precepts is emphasized in verse 93: "I will never forget thy precepts: for with them thou hast quickened me." This verse highlights the psalmist's determination to keep God's commandments at the forefront of his mind and life, recognizing that it is through these precepts that he has been "quickened," or made alive. The phrase "I will never forget" indicates a deep, personal commitment to continually remember and apply God's Word, acknowledging that it is the source of his spiritual vitality and discernment. This verse challenges us to consider the role of Scripture in our own lives. Do we, like the psalmist, make a deliberate effort to never forget God's precepts, recognizing them as the source of our spiritual life and discernment, or do we sometimes allow other priorities or distractions to cause us to neglect the importance of keeping God's Word central in our lives?

In verse 94, the psalmist expresses his total dependence on God's salvation and his commitment to seeking God's commandments: "I am thine, save me; for I have sought thy precepts." This verse reveals the psalmist's deep sense of belonging to God, which forms the basis for his plea for salvation. The phrase "I am thine" reflects the psalmist's identity as a servant of God, wholly committed to living according to His will. The request "save me" indicates the psalmist's recognition that only God can deliver him from his troubles, and his seeking of God's precepts shows that his desire for salvation is accompanied by a commitment to obedience. This verse challenges us to reflect on our own sense of identity and dependence on God. Do we, like the psalmist, recognize that we belong to God and seek His salvation through a commitment to His precepts, or do we sometimes rely on our own efforts or external solutions instead of fully entrusting our lives to God and His Word?

The psalmist's awareness of the threats posed by the wicked is evident in verse 95: "The wicked have waited for me to destroy me: but I will consider thy testimonies." This verse highlights the psalmist's recognition of the dangers he faces from those who seek to harm him, yet it also reveals his steadfast commitment to focusing on God's testimonies rather than being consumed by fear or anxiety. The phrase "but I will consider thy testimonies" indicates the psalmist's deliberate choice to prioritize the wisdom and guidance found in God's Word over the threats posed by his enemies. This verse challenges us to consider how we respond to the challenges and dangers we face in our own lives. Do we, like the psalmist, choose to focus on God's testimonies, finding discernment and strength in His Word, or do we allow fear and anxiety to distract us from the guidance that Scripture provides?

The passage concludes in verse 96 with a reflection on the limitations of all things, except for God's commandments: "I have seen an end of all perfection: but thy commandment is exceeding broad." This final verse encapsulates the psalmist's recognition that everything in the world has its limits—whether it be human achievements, knowledge, or power—yet God's commandments are limitless in their wisdom and scope. The phrase "exceeding broad" suggests that God's Word is boundless, offering guidance and discernment that extends far beyond the limitations of human understanding. This verse challenges us to consider the limitations of our own wisdom and the vastness of God's commandments. Do we, like the psalmist, recognize that true discernment comes from the limitless wisdom of God's Word, which far exceeds the confines of human knowledge and experience, or do we sometimes rely too heavily on our own understanding, neglecting the expansive guidance that Scripture provides?

As we explore the theme of discernment in Psalm 119, verses 89-96, we are reminded of the critical importance of grounding our decisions, actions, and understanding in the eternal truth of God's Word. The psalmist's example challenges us to consider how we approach our own need for discernment, especially in a world that is constantly changing and often unpredictable. Do we, like the psalmist, anchor our discernment in the unchanging, eternal Word of God, recognizing that it is the only source of wisdom that remains steadfast and reliable across all generations, or do we sometimes rely on the fleeting and often contradictory wisdom of the world?

Furthermore, the psalmist's emphasis on the life-sustaining power of God's Word, his commitment to remembering and obeying God's precepts, and his recognition of the limitless wisdom contained in God's commandments challenge us to deepen our own commitment to seeking discernment through Scripture. Are we willing to delight in God's Word, making it our source of strength and guidance during times of affliction? Do we remain steadfast in our commitment to

God's precepts, never forgetting their importance in our lives? And do we fully appreciate the breadth and depth of God's commandments, recognizing that they offer discernment and guidance that far surpasses anything the world can offer?

In conclusion, the theme of discernment in Psalm 119, verses 89-96, offers a powerful reminder of the need to anchor our lives in the eternal and unchanging truth of God's Word, especially when seeking wisdom and guidance in a complex and often confusing world. The psalmist's deep trust in the faithfulness of God's Word, his recognition of the life-giving power of Scripture, and his acknowledgment of the limitless wisdom contained in God's commandments challenge us to deepen our own commitment to seeking discernment through God's Word. As we continue to explore the depths of Psalm 119, may we be inspired to anchor our lives in the truth of Scripture, seeking the wisdom and discernment that comes from God's eternal Word, and recognizing that it is through our commitment to His commandments that we find the true purpose, guidance, and fulfillment we need to navigate the complexities and challenges of life.

Whether we are seeking to grow in our understanding of God's Word, striving to make wise and godly decisions, or facing the uncertainties and challenges of the world, may we always turn to His Word as our source of discernment and guidance, knowing that it is through our commitment to His commandments that we find the true wisdom and direction we need to live a life that is fully devoted to Him. The psalmist's example reminds us that true discernment is not found in human wisdom or in the shifting opinions of the world, but in the eternal and unchanging truth of God's Word. By placing our trust in God's Word and seeking His guidance in every aspect of our lives, we can experience the peace, strength, and fulfillment that come from living a life that is anchored in the truth of His commandments. As we continue to journey through Psalm 119, may we be encouraged to deepen our commitment to seeking discernment through God's Word, finding in it the strength, guidance, and inspiration we need to live a life that is fully devoted to Him, anchored in the truth of God's eternal Word.

Chapter 13 – The Dedication

In Psalm 119, verses 97-104, the theme of dedication is powerfully expressed as the psalmist pours out his deep love for God's law, recognizing that it provides wisdom and understanding far beyond what human teaching can offer. These verses offer a profound meditation on the joy, insight, and strength that come from a life fully dedicated to the study and application of God's Word. The psalmist begins in verse 97 with an exclamation of love and devotion: "O how love I thy law! it is my meditation all the day." This opening declaration sets the tone for the entire passage, highlighting the psalmist's deep affection for God's commandments. The phrase "O how love I thy law" is not merely a statement of appreciation but a passionate expression of the psalmist's unwavering dedication to the law of the Lord. The fact that he meditates on it "all the day" underscores the centrality of God's Word in his life, indicating that it is not just a part of his routine but the foundation upon which his thoughts, decisions, and actions are built. This verse challenges us to reflect on our own level of dedication to God's Word. Do we, like the psalmist, truly love God's law and make it the focus of our meditation throughout the day, allowing it to shape our lives in every aspect, or do we sometimes treat it as an afterthought, something we turn to only when it is convenient?

In verse 98, the psalmist continues by acknowledging the wisdom that comes from God's commandments: "Thou through thy commandments hast made me wiser than mine enemies: for they are ever with me." Here, the psalmist attributes his superior wisdom to his adherence to God's commandments, noting that this wisdom surpasses that of his enemies. The phrase "for they are ever with me" suggests that the psalmist constantly keeps God's commandments in mind, which equips him to navigate the challenges posed by those who oppose him. This verse highlights the practical benefits of dedicating oneself to God's Word, showing that it not only provides spiritual guidance but also gives one the discernment needed to overcome adversaries and obstacles. This verse challenges us to consider the source of our own wisdom. Do we, like the psalmist, rely on God's commandments to make us wiser than our enemies, or do we sometimes seek wisdom from other, less reliable sources that do not offer the same depth of insight?

The psalmist's dedication to God's Word is further emphasized in verse 99: "I have more understanding than all my teachers: for thy testimonies are my meditation." This verse reveals the psalmist's confidence in the understanding he has gained through his dedication to meditating on God's testimonies. The phrase "more understanding than all my teachers" suggests that the psalmist's commitment to God's Word has given him insight that surpasses even that of those who are supposed to instruct him. This verse underscores the idea that true understanding and wisdom come not from human knowledge alone, but from a deep engagement with the divine truths found in Scripture. This verse challenges us to reflect on where we seek understanding in our own lives. Do we, like the psalmist, prioritize the study and meditation of God's Word as the primary source of our understanding, or do we sometimes rely too heavily on human teachers and experts, neglecting the deeper wisdom that comes from Scripture?

In verse 100, the psalmist takes his reflection a step further, noting the maturity and discernment that come from following God's precepts: "I understand more than the ancients, because I keep thy precepts." Here, the psalmist contrasts his understanding with that of the "ancients," or elders, suggesting that his dedication to keeping God's precepts has given him insight that even those with more life experience may lack. The phrase "because I keep thy precepts" indicates that this understanding is not just theoretical but practical, gained through a life lived in obedience to God's commandments. This verse challenges us to consider the relationship between obedience and understanding in our own lives. Do we, like the psalmist, recognize that true discernment comes from not just knowing but keeping God's precepts, or do we sometimes separate our understanding from our actions, failing to live out the truths we have learned?

The psalmist's commitment to avoiding evil and staying true to God's Word is expressed in verse 101: "I have refrained my feet from every evil way, that I might keep thy word." This verse highlights the psalmist's determination to avoid sin and wrongdoing, motivated by his desire to remain faithful to God's Word. The phrase "refrained my feet" suggests a conscious, deliberate effort to steer clear of paths that would lead him away from God's commandments. This verse emphasizes the idea that dedication to God's Word involves not only pursuing what is right but also actively avoiding what is wrong. This verse challenges us to reflect on our own efforts to avoid evil in our lives. Do we, like the psalmist, make a deliberate effort to refrain from every evil way, motivated by a desire to keep God's Word, or do we sometimes allow ourselves to be drawn into actions or behaviors that are inconsistent with our faith?

In verse 102, the psalmist reaffirms his commitment to following God's laws, acknowledging the divine teaching he has received: "I have not departed from thy judgments: for thou hast taught me." This verse reflects the psalmist's recognition that his ability to stay true to God's judgments is not solely a result of his own efforts but is also due to the teaching and guidance he has received from God. The phrase "thou hast taught me" underscores the psalmist's humility and dependence on divine instruction, recognizing that his dedication to God's Word is rooted in God's own work in his life. This verse challenges us to consider the source of our own spiritual dedication. Do we, like the psalmist, acknowledge that our commitment to God's judgments is a result of His teaching and guidance, or do we sometimes take credit for our spiritual growth, forgetting the role that God's grace and instruction play in our lives?

The psalmist's expression of joy in God's commandments is beautifully captured in verse 103: "How sweet are thy words unto my taste! yea, sweeter than honey to my mouth!" This verse reveals the psalmist's deep delight in God's Word, comparing its sweetness to that of honey, a substance known for its pleasant and satisfying taste. The use of sensory language here—specifically the imagery of taste—emphasizes the personal and intimate nature of the psalmist's relationship with God's Word. This verse challenges us to consider the level of joy and satisfaction we find in Scripture. Do we, like the psalmist, experience God's Word as something sweet and delightful, something we eagerly consume and savor, or do we sometimes approach it as a duty or obligation, missing out on the deep pleasure it can bring?

The passage concludes in verse 104 with a declaration of the wisdom gained through God's precepts and a commitment to reject falsehood: "Through thy precepts I get understanding: therefore I hate every false way." This final verse encapsulates the psalmist's journey of dedication, highlighting the understanding that has come from studying and living by God's precepts. The phrase "therefore I hate every false way" reflects the psalmist's strong rejection of anything that is contrary to the truth of God's Word, showing that his dedication has not only given him wisdom but also shaped his values and commitments. This verse challenges us to consider the impact of God's precepts on our own understanding and values. Do we, like the psalmist, gain understanding through our dedication to God's precepts, leading us to reject falsehood and embrace truth, or do we sometimes struggle to discern and reject the false ways that are presented to us by the world?

As we explore the theme of dedication in Psalm 119, verses 97-104, we are reminded of the profound impact that a deep love for and commitment to God's Word can have on our lives. The psalmist's example challenges us to consider how we approach our relationship with Scripture, especially in terms of our dedication to studying, meditating on, and living out its teachings. Do we, like the psalmist, truly love God's law and make it the focus of our daily meditation, allowing it to shape every aspect of our lives, or do we sometimes neglect the importance of dedicating ourselves fully to the study and application of God's Word?

Furthermore, the psalmist's recognition of the wisdom and understanding that come from God's commandments, his commitment to avoiding evil and staying true to God's precepts, and his deep delight in the sweetness of God's Word challenge us to deepen our own dedication to living according to Scripture. Are we willing to prioritize the study and meditation of God's Word as the primary source of our wisdom and understanding? Do we make a deliberate effort to refrain from every evil way, motivated by a desire to keep God's Word? And do we experience the joy and satisfaction that come from savoring the sweetness of God's commandments, allowing them to shape our values and guide our decisions?

In conclusion, the theme of dedication in Psalm 119, verses 97-104, offers a powerful reminder of the need to anchor our lives in a deep and abiding love for God's Word, recognizing that it is through our dedication to His commandments that we find true wisdom, understanding, and fulfillment. The psalmist's unwavering commitment to God's Word, his recognition of the divine teaching he has received, and his rejection of falsehood challenge us to deepen our own dedication to living according to God's commandments. As we continue to explore the depths of Psalm 119, may we be inspired to reaffirm our commitment to God's Word, seeking the wisdom and understanding that come

from a life fully dedicated to His commandments, and recognizing that it is through our love for and meditation on His Word that we find the true purpose, guidance, and fulfillment we need to navigate the complexities and challenges of life.

Whether we are seeking to grow in our understanding of God's Word, striving to live a life that honors God, or facing the challenges and temptations of the world, may we always turn to His Word as our source of wisdom, guidance, and inspiration, knowing that it is through our dedication to His commandments that we find the true purpose and direction we need to live a life that is fully devoted to Him. The psalmist's example reminds us that true dedication is not just about knowing God's Word, but about loving it, meditating on it, and allowing it to shape every aspect of our lives. By placing our trust in God's Word and seeking His guidance in every aspect of our lives, we can experience the peace, strength, and fulfillment that come from living a life that is anchored in the truth of His commandments. As we continue to journey through Psalm 119, may we be encouraged to deepen our dedication to God's Word, finding in it the wisdom, guidance, and inspiration we need to live a life that is fully devoted to Him, anchored in the truth of God's eternal Word.

Chapter 14 – The Direction

In Psalm 119, verses 105-112, the theme of direction is deeply explored as the psalmist reflects on how God's Word serves as a lamp and a light, guiding his path and shaping the choices he makes in life. These verses vividly illustrate the psalmist's reliance on the guidance provided by Scripture, highlighting the importance of divine direction in navigating the complexities and challenges of life. The psalmist begins in verse 105 with a declaration that has become one of the most well-known and beloved verses in all of Scripture: "Thy word is a lamp unto my feet, and a light unto my path." This opening verse sets the tone for the entire passage, expressing the psalmist's recognition that without the light of God's Word, he would be lost in the darkness, unsure of which way to turn. The metaphor of God's Word as a lamp and a light suggests that Scripture provides both immediate guidance ("unto my feet") and long-term direction ("unto my path"), ensuring that the psalmist can see clearly where he is going and make decisions that align with God's will. This verse challenges us to consider how we view the role of Scripture in our own lives. Do we, like the psalmist, rely on God's Word as our primary source of direction, trusting it to guide our steps and illuminate the path ahead, or do we sometimes attempt to navigate life's challenges on our own, without the benefit of the divine light that Scripture provides?

In verse 106, the psalmist makes a solemn commitment to follow the direction given by God's Word: "I have sworn, and I will perform it, that I will keep thy righteous judgments." This verse highlights the psalmist's determination to live in accordance with God's commands, emphasizing that his commitment is not just a casual intention, but a sworn oath that he fully intends to carry out. The phrase "I will perform it" underscores the psalmist's resolve to actively live out the righteous judgments found in Scripture, rather than merely acknowledging them in theory. This verse challenges us to reflect on the seriousness of our own commitment to following God's direction. Do we, like the psalmist, make firm commitments to obey God's Word, and then actively follow through on those commitments, or do we sometimes make promises to God that we fail to keep, allowing our dedication to waver in the face of difficulty or temptation?

The psalmist's reliance on God's direction is further emphasized in verse 107, where he cries out in the midst of affliction: "I am afflicted very much: quicken me, O Lord, according unto thy word." This verse reveals the psalmist's dependence on God's Word for life and strength, especially during times of intense suffering. The use of the word "quicken" suggests that the psalmist is seeking revival or renewal, asking God to breathe new life into him according to the promises of Scripture. The acknowledgment of being "afflicted very much" underscores the depth of the psalmist's struggles, yet even in his darkest moments, he turns to God's Word for the direction and sustenance he needs to persevere. This verse challenges us to consider where we turn when we are faced with affliction. Do we, like the psalmist, seek renewal and strength through the promises of God's Word, trusting that it will guide us through even the most difficult circumstances, or do we sometimes look elsewhere for comfort and direction, missing out on the life-giving power of Scripture?

In verse 108, the psalmist offers a prayer that reflects his desire to live a life directed by God's Word: "Accept, I beseech thee, the freewill offerings of my mouth, O Lord, and teach me thy judgments." This verse highlights the psalmist's willingness to offer praise and thanksgiving to God, not out of obligation, but as a voluntary expression of his devotion. The phrase "freewill offerings of my mouth" suggests that the psalmist's words of praise are given freely and joyfully, reflecting a heart that is fully committed to following God's direction. The request "teach me thy judgments" further emphasizes the psalmist's desire for ongoing instruction and guidance from God's Word, recognizing that he still has much to learn and that his life's direction depends on continued growth in understanding. This verse challenges us to examine our own attitude toward worship and learning. Do we, like the psalmist, offer our praise to God freely and joyfully, and seek to continually learn and be directed by His judgments, or do we sometimes approach worship and study as mere duties, without the deep desire for guidance and growth that the psalmist expresses?

The psalmist's acknowledgment of the dangers he faces and his reliance on God's Word for protection and direction is evident in verse 109: "My soul is continually in my hand: yet do I not forget thy law." This verse reveals the precariousness of the psalmist's situation, as he describes his life as being constantly at risk ("continually in my hand"). Despite the ever-present danger, the psalmist remains committed to not forgetting God's law, indicating that he sees God's Word as his ultimate source of protection and guidance, even in the face of mortal threats. The phrase "yet do I not forget thy law" suggests that the psalmist's dedication to following God's direction remains unshaken, regardless of the external circumstances. This verse challenges us to consider how we respond to danger and uncertainty in our own lives. Do we, like the psalmist, cling to God's Word as our source of direction and protection, even when our lives are at risk, or do we allow fear and anxiety to cause us to forget or neglect the guidance that Scripture provides?

In verse 110, the psalmist describes the snares that have been set for him by the wicked, and his determination to stay true to God's direction: "The wicked have laid a snare for me: yet I erred not from thy precepts." This verse highlights the reality of the psalmist's enemies and the traps they have set in an attempt to lead him astray or cause him harm. Despite these dangers, the psalmist remains resolute in his commitment to follow God's precepts, refusing to be led off course by the schemes of the wicked. The phrase "yet I erred not from thy precepts" underscores the psalmist's unwavering dedication to staying on the path that God's Word has laid out for him, regardless of the obstacles or temptations he encounters. This verse challenges us to reflect on our own commitment to following God's direction when we face opposition or temptation. Do we, like the psalmist, remain steadfast in our adherence to God's precepts, refusing to be led astray by the snares of the wicked, or do we sometimes allow ourselves to be diverted from the path of righteousness by the pressures and enticements of the world?

The psalmist's deep love for God's Word and his recognition of its value as an eternal inheritance is expressed in verse 111: "Thy testimonies have I taken as an heritage for ever: for they are the rejoicing of my heart." This verse reflects the psalmist's view of God's testimonies as his most treasured possession, something that he has "taken as an heritage for ever." The use of the word "heritage" suggests that the psalmist sees God's Word as an inheritance that is not only valuable in this life but also eternal, something that will continue to guide and bless him for all time. The phrase "the rejoicing of my heart" indicates that the psalmist finds deep joy and satisfaction in the direction provided by God's Word, viewing it as a source of true happiness and fulfillment. This verse challenges us to consider how we value and cherish God's Word in our own lives. Do we, like the psalmist, view Scripture as our most precious inheritance, something that brings joy and rejoicing to our hearts, or do we sometimes take it for granted, failing to recognize the eternal value and guidance it offers?

The passage concludes in verse 112 with a final affirmation of the psalmist's dedication to following God's direction: "I have inclined mine heart to perform thy statutes alway, even unto the end." This concluding verse encapsulates the psalmist's unwavering commitment to living according to God's statutes, not just for a season, but "alway, even unto the end." The phrase "inclined mine heart" suggests that the psalmist has made a deliberate, conscious choice to align his heart and will with God's Word, committing to follow His direction for the entirety of his life. This verse challenges us to reflect on the longevity and consistency of our own dedication to following God's direction. Do we, like the psalmist, incline our hearts to perform God's statutes consistently and faithfully, with the intention of doing so "even unto the end," or do we sometimes allow our commitment to waver, following God's direction only when it is convenient or aligns with our own desires?

As we explore the theme of direction in Psalm 119, verses 105-112, we are reminded of the crucial role that God's Word plays in guiding our lives and shaping our choices. The psalmist's example challenges us to consider how we approach the guidance provided by Scripture, especially in terms of our dedication to following the path that God's Word has illuminated for us. Do we, like the psalmist, rely on God's Word as our primary source of direction, trusting it to guide our steps and illuminate the path ahead, or do we sometimes attempt to navigate life's challenges on our own, without the benefit of the divine light that Scripture provides?

Furthermore, the psalmist's recognition of the life-giving power of God's Word, his commitment to following God's direction even in the face of affliction and danger, and his deep love for the testimonies that serve as his eternal heritage challenge us to deepen our own dedication to living according to Scripture. Are we willing to make firm commitments to obey God's Word and then actively follow through on those commitments, trusting that God's direction will lead us through even the most difficult circumstances? Do we view God's Word as our most treasured possession, something that brings joy and rejoicing to our hearts, and are we committed to following its direction consistently and faithfully, "even unto the end"?

In conclusion, the theme of direction in Psalm 119, verses 105-112, offers a powerful reminder of the need to anchor our lives in the guidance provided by God's Word, recognizing that it is through our dedication to His commandments that we find true wisdom, understanding, and fulfillment. The psalmist's unwavering commitment to following God's direction, his recognition of the divine light that Scripture provides, and his deep love for the testimonies that serve as his eternal heritage challenge us to deepen our own dedication to living according to God's commandments. As we continue to explore the depths of Psalm 119, may we be inspired to reaffirm our commitment to God's Word, seeking the guidance and direction that come from a life fully dedicated to His commandments, and recognizing that it is through our reliance on Scripture that we find the true purpose, guidance, and fulfillment we need to navigate the complexities and challenges of life. Whether we are seeking to grow in our understanding of God's Word, striving to live a life that honors God, or facing the challenges and temptations of the world, may we always turn to His Word as our source of direction, guidance, and inspiration, knowing that it is through our dedication to His commandments that we find the true purpose and direction we need to live a life that is fully devoted to Him. The psalmist's example reminds us that true direction is not found in human wisdom or in the shifting opinions of the world, but in the eternal and unchanging truth of God's Word. By placing our trust in God's Word and seeking His guidance in every aspect of our lives, we can experience the peace, strength, and fulfillment that come from living a life that is anchored in the truth of His commandments. As we continue to journey through Psalm 119, may we be encouraged to deepen our commitment to seeking direction through God's Word, finding in it the strength, guidance, and inspiration we need to live a life that is fully devoted to Him, anchored in the truth of God's eternal Word.

Chapter 15 – The Distress

In Psalm 119, verses 113-120, the theme of distress is poignantly captured as the psalmist cries out to God for help and protection in times of great turmoil, while reaffirming his unwavering commitment to God's statutes. These verses looks deeply into the emotional and spiritual struggles that accompany distress, yet they also highlight the psalmist's resolute faith in the power of God's Word to provide comfort, guidance, and deliverance. The passage begins in verse 113 with a bold declaration: "I hate vain thoughts: but thy law do I love." Here, the psalmist contrasts the futility of "vain thoughts"—those that are empty, deceitful, or without purpose—with the solid, enduring truth of God's law. This opening verse sets the stage for the psalmist's plea for help, establishing that his distress is not merely a result of external pressures, but also a response to the internal battle between meaningless thoughts and the love he holds for God's commandments. The phrase "thy law do I love" signifies that even in the midst of mental and emotional turmoil, the psalmist remains deeply devoted to God's Word, finding in it a steadfast anchor for his soul. This verse challenges us to consider how we manage our own thoughts in times of distress. Do we, like the psalmist, reject the vain, distracting thoughts that threaten to overwhelm us and instead focus on the unchanging truth of God's law, or do we allow our minds to be consumed by worries and doubts, losing sight of the comfort and direction that Scripture provides?

In verse 114, the psalmist continues by expressing his reliance on God as a refuge: "Thou art my hiding place and my shield: I hope in thy word." This verse encapsulates the psalmist's deep trust in God's protection and his commitment to finding security in God's promises. The metaphors of God as a "hiding place" and a "shield" vividly convey the psalmist's sense of safety and defense against the dangers and threats that surround him. The phrase "I hope in thy word" underscores the source of this security—God's Word, which the psalmist clings to as a beacon of hope in the darkest of times. This verse challenges us to reflect on where we seek refuge in our moments of distress. Do we, like the psalmist, turn to God as our hiding place and shield, placing our hope in the promises of His Word, or do we sometimes look to other sources of security that ultimately fail to provide the protection and peace we need?

The psalmist's plea for God's intervention is further emphasized in verse 115: "Depart from me, ye evildoers: for I will keep the commandments of my God." This verse reveals the psalmist's determination to distance himself from those who seek to lead him astray or harm him, and his commitment to remain faithful to God's commandments despite the pressures of the wicked. The command "Depart from me, ye evildoers" signifies the psalmist's refusal to associate with or be influenced by those who do not follow God's ways. The resolve to "keep the commandments of my God" highlights the psalmist's unwavering dedication to living according to God's Word, even when surrounded by those who oppose or mock his faith. This verse challenges us to consider how we respond to the presence of evil and temptation in our own lives. Do we, like the psalmist, boldly reject the influence of evildoers and remain committed to keeping God's commandments, or do we sometimes allow ourselves to be swayed by the negative influences around us, compromising our dedication to God's Word?

In verse 116, the psalmist makes a heartfelt appeal for God's sustaining grace: "Uphold me according unto thy word, that I may live: and let me not be ashamed of my hope." This verse captures the psalmist's recognition that his very life depends on God's support, and that without divine upholding, he would falter under the weight of his distress. The request to be "upheld according unto thy word" emphasizes the psalmist's belief that God's promises are the foundation of his strength and survival. The plea "let me not be ashamed of my hope" reflects the psalmist's desire to remain confident in his trust in God, even when circumstances might tempt him to doubt or feel embarrassed about his faith. This verse challenges us to consider the source of our own strength in times of distress. Do we, like the psalmist, rely on God's Word to uphold us and sustain our hope, trusting that we will not be put to shame for our faith, or do we sometimes struggle to maintain our confidence in God's promises when faced with overwhelming challenges?

The psalmist's acknowledgment of his vulnerability and dependence on God's mercy is evident in verse 117: "Hold thou me up, and I shall be safe: and I will have respect unto thy statutes continually." This verse echoes the themes of the previous verse, further emphasizing the psalmist's need for God's sustaining power. The phrase "Hold thou me up, and I shall be safe" reflects the psalmist's complete reliance on God for protection and security, acknowledging that only through divine support can he remain safe from harm. The commitment to "have respect unto thy statutes continually" indicates that the psalmist's dedication to God's commandments is not a temporary or conditional response to distress, but a lifelong commitment to following God's ways. This verse challenges us to reflect on our own sense of security and our dedication to God's Word. Do we, like the psalmist, recognize that our safety and well-being depend on God's sustaining power, and do we remain committed to respecting and following His statutes continually, or do we sometimes waver in our dedication when we feel vulnerable or uncertain?

In verse 118, the psalmist reflects on the fate of those who reject God's direction: "Thou hast trodden down all them that err from thy statutes: for their deceit is falsehood." This verse reveals the psalmist's understanding that those who stray from God's commandments and rely on deceit and falsehood will ultimately be brought low. The phrase "thou hast trodden down" suggests a decisive and final judgment against those who err from God's statutes, emphasizing the futility and destructiveness of living apart from God's truth. The recognition that "their deceit is falsehood" underscores the psalmist's belief that anything built on lies and deception is doomed to fail. This verse challenges us to consider the consequences of rejecting God's direction in our own lives. Do we, like the psalmist, understand that straying from God's commandments and embracing deceit will ultimately lead to our downfall, or do we sometimes underestimate the seriousness of living in opposition to God's truth?

The psalmist's reverence for God and his recognition of the fleeting nature of those who oppose God's ways is expressed in verse 119: "Thou puttest away all the wicked of the earth like dross: therefore I love thy testimonies." This verse uses the metaphor of dross—the impurities removed from metal during the refining process—to describe the fate of the wicked, who are discarded and removed by God. The psalmist's observation that God "puttest away all the wicked of the earth" reflects his belief in divine justice and the ultimate triumph of righteousness. The phrase "therefore I love thy testimonies" indicates that the psalmist's love for God's Word is reinforced by his understanding of God's righteous judgment and the impermanence of wickedness. This verse challenges us to reflect on our own love for God's testimonies and our understanding of His justice. Do we, like the psalmist, love God's Word all the more because we recognize the justice and righteousness of His ways, and do we trust that He will ultimately remove the wicked like dross, or do we sometimes struggle to reconcile the presence of wickedness with our faith in God's justice?

The passage concludes in verse 120 with a powerful expression of reverent fear: "My flesh trembleth for fear of thee; and I am afraid of thy judgments." This final verse encapsulates the psalmist's deep awe and reverence for God, recognizing the seriousness and weight of divine judgment. The phrase "My flesh trembleth for fear of thee" suggests a visceral, physical reaction to the awareness of God's power and holiness, indicating that the psalmist's reverence is not just intellectual but deeply felt. The admission "I am afraid of thy judgments" reflects the psalmist's understanding that God's judgments are righteous and just, and that they should be approached with the utmost respect and seriousness. This verse challenges us to consider our own attitude toward God's judgments. Do we, like the psalmist, approach God with a reverent fear, recognizing the gravity and holiness of His judgments, or do we sometimes take His commandments and decisions lightly, failing to fully grasp the significance of divine justice?

As we explore the theme of distress in Psalm 119, verses 113-120, we are reminded of the importance of turning to God in our times of greatest need, while maintaining a steadfast commitment to His Word. The psalmist's example challenges us to consider how we respond to distress, both internally and externally, especially in terms of our reliance on God's protection and our dedication to following His commandments. Do we, like the psalmist, cry out to God for help and protection, trusting in His Word to guide us through our distress, or do we sometimes allow fear and anxiety to drive us away from the very source of our comfort and security?

Furthermore, the psalmist's unwavering commitment to God's statutes, his rejection of deceit and evil, and his deep reverence for God's judgments challenge us to deepen our own dedication to living according to Scripture. Are we willing to distance ourselves from those who seek to lead us astray, and to uphold God's commandments even in the face of opposition? Do we recognize the importance of relying on God's sustaining power, and do we approach His judgments with the reverent fear that they deserve?

In conclusion, the theme of distress in Psalm 119, verses 113-120, offers a powerful reminder of the need to anchor our lives in the protection and guidance provided by God's Word, especially in times of turmoil and uncertainty. The psalmist's unwavering commitment to following God's direction, his reliance on divine protection, and his deep reverence for God's judgments challenge us to deepen our own dedication to living according to Scripture. As we continue to explore the depths of Psalm 119, may we be inspired to reaffirm our commitment to God's Word, seeking the protection and direction that come from a life fully dedicated to His commandments, and recognizing that it is through our reliance on Scripture that we find the true strength, guidance, and peace we need to navigate the complexities and challenges of life.

Whether we are seeking to grow in our understanding of God's Word, striving to live a life that honors God, or facing the challenges and temptations of the world, may we always turn to His Word as our source of protection, guidance, and inspiration, knowing that it is through our dedication to His commandments that we find the true purpose and direction we need to live a life that is fully devoted to Him. The psalmist's example reminds us that true protection and direction are not found in human wisdom or in the shifting circumstances of the world, but in the eternal and unchanging truth of God's Word. By placing our trust in God's Word and seeking His protection in every aspect of our lives, we can experience the peace, strength, and fulfillment that come from living a life that is anchored in the truth of His commandments. As we continue to journey through Psalm 119, may we be encouraged to deepen our commitment to seeking protection and direction through God's Word, finding in it the strength, guidance, and inspiration we need to live a life that is fully devoted to Him, anchored in the truth of God's eternal Word.

Chapter 16 – The Deliverance

In Psalm 119, verses 121-128 of the Word of God, the theme of deliverance is powerfully explored as the psalmist pleads for God's intervention in the face of oppression while simultaneously declaring the rightness and righteousness of God's commands. These verses reveal the psalmist's deep reliance on God's justice and his unwavering belief that deliverance comes through a steadfast commitment to the truths found in Scripture. The passage begins in verse 121 with a bold assertion of integrity: "I have done judgment and justice: leave me not to mine oppressors." This opening verse sets the tone for the psalmist's plea, highlighting his dedication to living a life of righteousness and justice. The phrase "I have done judgment and justice" suggests that the psalmist has lived in accordance with God's laws, striving to act fairly and justly in all his dealings. Yet, despite his commitment to righteousness, he finds himself under the threat of oppression, and his cry, "leave me not to mine oppressors," reflects his urgent need for God's deliverance. This verse challenges us to consider how we respond when we face injustice or oppression, especially when we believe we have acted rightly. Do we, like the psalmist, trust in God's ability to deliver us, even when our circumstances seem overwhelming, or do we sometimes falter in our faith, feeling abandoned or powerless in the face of oppression?

In verse 122, the psalmist continues by making a heartfelt appeal for God's protection: "Be surety for thy servant for good: let not the proud oppress me." This verse introduces the concept of God as a "surety" or guarantor, someone who takes responsibility for the well-being of the psalmist. The request for God to be a surety "for good" reflects the psalmist's deep desire for divine intervention, asking God to ensure that his life is marked by goodness and protection rather than suffering at the hands of the proud. The plea "let not the proud oppress me" highlights the psalmist's awareness of the arrogance and cruelty of those who seek to harm him, and his trust that God's intervention can prevent their oppression. This verse challenges us to consider where we seek protection and assurance in our own lives. Do we, like the psalmist, ask God to be our surety, trusting in His power to protect us from those who would oppress us, or do we sometimes rely on our own strength or the assurances of others, forgetting that true deliverance comes from God alone?

The psalmist's longing for divine action is further emphasized in verse 123: "Mine eyes fail for thy salvation, and for the word of thy righteousness." This verse vividly conveys the psalmist's deep yearning for God's deliverance, to the point where his eyes are "failing" from watching and waiting. The phrase "mine eyes fail" suggests that the psalmist has been eagerly anticipating God's salvation for so long that he is physically and emotionally exhausted. Yet, even in this state of weariness, he remains focused on "the word of thy righteousness," indicating his belief that God's deliverance is rooted in His just and righteous character. This verse challenges us to reflect on our own persistence in seeking God's deliverance. Do we, like the psalmist, continue to look for God's salvation with unwavering faith, even when the wait is long and arduous, or do we sometimes grow weary and lose hope, forgetting that God's timing and righteousness are perfect?

In verse 124, the psalmist makes a plea for mercy and continued instruction: "Deal with thy servant according unto thy mercy, and teach me thy statutes." This verse reflects the psalmist's recognition that his need for deliverance is not based solely on his own righteousness, but also on God's mercy. The request to be dealt with "according unto thy mercy" indicates a humble acknowledgment that the psalmist relies on God's grace and compassion, rather than on his own merit, to receive the deliverance he seeks. Additionally, the psalmist's desire to be taught God's statutes emphasizes that even in his distress, he remains committed to growing in his understanding of God's Word, recognizing that true deliverance comes not just from being rescued from oppression, but from being continually guided by God's laws. This verse challenges us to consider our own reliance on God's mercy and our commitment to learning from His Word. Do we, like the psalmist, approach God with humility, seeking His mercy and desiring to be taught His statutes, or do we sometimes focus only on the immediate need for deliverance, neglecting the ongoing instruction and growth that God desires for us?

The psalmist's plea for understanding and the acknowledgment of God's commands as the foundation of life is expressed in verse 125: "I am thy servant; give me understanding, that I may know thy testimonies." This verse highlights the psalmist's identity as a servant of God, committed to doing His will and following His commands. The request for understanding suggests that the psalmist recognizes the need for divine wisdom to fully comprehend and live out God's testimonies. The phrase "that I may know thy testimonies" indicates that the psalmist's desire for understanding is not merely intellectual, but deeply practical—he wants to know God's Word so that he can apply it faithfully in his life. This verse challenges us to reflect on our own pursuit of understanding and how it relates to our role as servants of God. Do we, like the psalmist, seek understanding from God with the intention of knowing and living out His testimonies, or do we sometimes approach Scripture as a mere academic exercise, without the deep desire to apply its truths in our daily lives?

In verse 126, the psalmist boldly calls for divine intervention, recognizing the urgency of the situation: "It is time for thee, Lord, to work: for they have made void thy law." This verse reflects the psalmist's sense of urgency and his belief that the time has come for God to take action. The phrase "It is time for thee, Lord, to work" suggests that the psalmist sees the situation as reaching a critical point, where only God's intervention can rectify the wrongs that have been done. The observation that "they have made void thy law" highlights the psalmist's concern that God's commandments are being ignored or violated by those who oppress him, and his belief that this requires a decisive response from God. This verse challenges us to consider how we respond when we see God's laws being disregarded or trampled upon. Do we, like the psalmist, call out to God for intervention, trusting that He will act to uphold His Word and deliver those who are oppressed, or do we sometimes remain silent or passive, failing to seek God's deliverance in the face of injustice?

The psalmist's love for God's commandments and his recognition of their value is powerfully expressed in verse 127: "Therefore I love thy commandments above gold; yea, above fine gold." This verse reflects the psalmist's deep affection for God's Word, which he values more highly than the most precious earthly treasures. The comparison to "gold" and "fine gold" underscores the idea that the psalmist sees God's commandments as the ultimate source of wealth and prosperity, far surpassing any material riches. The use of the word "therefore" suggests that the psalmist's love for God's commandments is directly connected to his belief in their righteousness and their ability to bring deliverance. This verse challenges us to reflect on what we value most in our own lives. Do we, like the psalmist, love God's commandments above all else, recognizing them as more valuable than any earthly possession, or do we sometimes allow the pursuit of material wealth or other worldly desires to take precedence over our love for God's Word?

The passage concludes in verse 128 with a firm declaration of the rightness of God's precepts and a rejection of falsehood: "Therefore I esteem all thy precepts concerning all things to be right; and I hate every false way." This final verse encapsulates the psalmist's unwavering commitment to God's Word, declaring that he esteems—or holds in the highest regard—all of God's precepts as being right and true. The phrase "concerning all things" suggests that the psalmist sees God's precepts as universally applicable, providing the correct guidance for every aspect of life. The strong statement "I hate every false way" reflects the psalmist's rejection of anything that is contrary to God's truth, underscoring his dedication to living in accordance with God's righteous commands. This verse challenges us to consider our own attitude toward God's precepts and our response to falsehood. Do we, like the psalmist, esteem all of God's precepts as being right and true, and do we actively reject every false way, or do we sometimes compromise on the truth, allowing falsehood to creep into our lives or our beliefs?

As we explore the theme of deliverance in Psalm 119, verses 121-128, we are reminded of the importance of seeking God's intervention and protection in times of oppression, while also maintaining a steadfast commitment to the rightness of His commands. The psalmist's example challenges us to consider how we respond when we face injustice or oppression, especially in terms of our reliance on God's deliverance and our dedication to living according to His Word. Do we, like the psalmist, cry out to God for deliverance, trusting in His righteousness and justice, even when the situation seems dire, or do we sometimes falter in our faith, feeling overwhelmed or defeated by the challenges we face?

Furthermore, the psalmist's recognition of the value of God's commandments, his desire for understanding, and his rejection of falsehood challenge us to deepen our own commitment to living according to Scripture. Are we willing to seek understanding from God with the intention of applying His precepts in every area of our lives? Do we value God's commandments above all else, recognizing their worth as greater than any material possession? And do we actively reject every false way, remaining steadfast in our commitment to the truth of God's Word?

In conclusion, the theme of deliverance in Psalm 119, verses 121-128, offers a powerful reminder of the need to anchor our lives in the righteousness and justice of God's Word, especially when seeking protection and deliverance from oppression. The psalmist's unwavering commitment to God's commands, his plea for divine intervention, and his recognition of the value of God's Word challenge us to deepen our own dedication to living according to Scripture. As we continue to explore the depths of Psalm 119, may we be inspired to reaffirm our commitment to God's Word, seeking the deliverance and protection that come from a life fully dedicated to His commandments, and recognizing that it is through our reliance on Scripture that we find the true strength, guidance, and peace we need to navigate the complexities and challenges of life.

Whether we are seeking to grow in our understanding of God's Word, striving to live a life that honors God, or facing the challenges and temptations of the world, may we always turn to His Word as our source of deliverance, guidance, and inspiration, knowing that it is through our dedication to His commandments that we find the true purpose and direction we need to live a life that is fully devoted to Him. The psalmist's example reminds us that true deliverance is not found in human strength or in the shifting circumstances of the world, but in the eternal and unchanging truth of God's Word. By placing our trust in God's Word and seeking His deliverance in every aspect of our lives, we can experience the peace, strength, and fulfillment that come from living a life that is anchored in the truth of His commandments. As we continue to journey through Psalm 119, may we be encouraged to deepen our commitment to seeking deliverance and protection through God's Word, finding in it the strength, guidance, and inspiration we need to live a life that is fully devoted to Him, anchored in the truth of God's eternal Word.

Chapter 17 – The Dedication

In Psalm 119, verses 129-136, the theme of dedication is explored with profound intensity as the psalmist renews his commitment to keeping God's precepts, while also expressing a deep longing for others to follow His ways. These verses reveal the psalmist's heartfelt devotion to the Word of God, coupled with a passionate desire for the world around him to embrace the same truth and light that guides his life. The passage begins in verse 129 with an exclamation of awe: "Thy testimonies are wonderful: therefore doth my soul keep them." This verse sets the tone for the psalmist's renewed dedication, highlighting the wonder and beauty he finds in God's testimonies. The word "wonderful" captures the psalmist's deep admiration for the divine laws, which he sees as perfect, just, and awe-inspiring. Because of their greatness, the psalmist's soul is compelled to keep them, indicating that his obedience is not born out of mere duty, but out of genuine reverence and love for God's Word. This verse challenges us to reflect on our own dedication to God's precepts. Do we, like the psalmist, find God's testimonies so wonderful that our souls are naturally inclined to keep them, or do we sometimes approach obedience as a burden, missing the beauty and majesty that the psalmist sees in God's commands?

In verse 130, the psalmist continues by highlighting the enlightening power of God's Word: "The entrance of thy words giveth light; it giveth understanding unto the simple." Here, the psalmist acknowledges that God's Word has the power to bring light into the darkest corners of our lives, offering clarity and understanding to all who seek it. The phrase "the entrance of thy words" suggests that when we allow God's Word to enter our hearts and minds, it illuminates our path, revealing truth and wisdom that may have previously been hidden from us. The psalmist emphasizes that this light is available even to "the simple," meaning that God's wisdom is accessible to all, regardless of their intellectual or spiritual status. This verse challenges us to consider how we approach God's Word. Do we, like the psalmist, invite the entrance of God's words into our lives, allowing them to shed light on our decisions, thoughts, and actions, or do we sometimes resist or neglect the light that Scripture offers, preferring to rely on our own understanding?

The psalmist's deep longing for God's commandments is vividly expressed in verse 131: "I opened my mouth, and panted: for I longed for thy commandments." This verse uses the imagery of thirst and longing to convey the psalmist's intense desire for God's Word. The act of opening the mouth and panting suggests a desperate need, as if the psalmist is parched and in need of refreshment, and that refreshment can only be found in God's commandments. The word "longed" indicates that this is not a casual or passing interest, but a deep, soul-level yearning for the guidance and wisdom that God's commandments provide. This verse challenges us to reflect on the intensity of our own desire for God's Word. Do we, like the psalmist, experience a deep, almost physical longing for God's commandments, seeking them out as the source of our spiritual nourishment, or do we sometimes take them for granted, failing to recognize our need for the guidance and wisdom they offer?

In verse 132, the psalmist makes a heartfelt plea for God's mercy: "Look thou upon me, and be merciful unto me, as thou usest to do unto those that love thy name." This verse reflects the psalmist's recognition of his dependence on God's mercy, acknowledging that any favor he receives is not due to his own merit, but to God's gracious nature. The request for God to "look upon" him indicates a desire for divine attention and care, while the phrase "as thou usest to do" suggests that the psalmist is appealing to God's established character, confident that God's mercy is consistent and reliable. This verse challenges us to consider how we approach God in our need. Do we, like the psalmist, humbly ask for God's mercy, trusting in His consistent and loving nature, or do we sometimes feel entitled to His favor, forgetting that it is only by His grace that we receive His blessings?

The psalmist's commitment to living according to God's Word is further emphasized in verse 133: "Order my steps in thy word: and let not any iniquity have dominion over me." This verse reveals the psalmist's desire for God to guide every aspect of his life, asking for his steps to be "ordered" or directed according to God's Word. The psalmist recognizes that only by walking in alignment with Scripture can he avoid the pitfalls of sin and iniquity. The phrase "let not any iniquity have dominion over me" reflects a fear of being controlled or overpowered by sin, and a plea for God's help in maintaining a life of righteousness. This verse challenges us to examine how we seek guidance in our own lives. Do we, like the psalmist, ask God to order our steps according to His Word, striving to live in a way that is free from the dominion of sin, or do we sometimes neglect the discipline required to walk in God's ways, allowing iniquity to gain a foothold in our lives?

In verse 134, the psalmist pleads for deliverance from the oppression of others: "Deliver me from the oppression of man: so will I keep thy precepts." This verse highlights the psalmist's recognition that external pressures and oppression can threaten his ability to live according to God's precepts. The request for deliverance from the oppression of man indicates that the psalmist is experiencing significant opposition or persecution, and he understands that only God's intervention can provide the freedom he needs to continue faithfully following God's commands. The phrase "so will I keep thy precepts" suggests that the psalmist's primary concern is not just personal safety or comfort, but the ability to remain obedient to God in the face of challenges. This verse challenges us to consider how we respond to external pressures that threaten our spiritual integrity. Do we, like the psalmist, seek God's deliverance so that we can continue to keep His precepts, prioritizing our obedience to Him over our desire for relief from oppression, or do we sometimes compromise our faith in response to the pressures we face?

The psalmist's deep desire for God's favor is expressed in verse 135: "Make thy face to shine upon thy servant; and teach me thy statutes." This verse uses the imagery of God's face shining upon the psalmist to convey a sense of divine favor, blessing, and presence. The psalmist longs for the light of God's countenance, understanding that this is the ultimate source of guidance and joy. The request to be taught God's statutes indicates that the psalmist sees the knowledge of God's Word as a crucial part of experiencing His favor. This verse challenges us to reflect on our own desire for God's presence and instruction. Do we, like the psalmist, long for God's face to shine upon us, seeking His favor and the joy that comes from being in His presence, and do we recognize that this favor is intimately connected with learning and following His statutes?

The passage concludes in verse 136 with a powerful expression of grief for those who do not follow God's law: "Rivers of waters run down mine eyes, because they keep not thy law." This final verse reveals the psalmist's deep sorrow for the disobedience of others, indicating that his dedication to God's Word is not only personal but also extends to a heartfelt concern for the spiritual well-being of others. The imagery of "rivers of waters" running down his eyes suggests intense weeping and mourning, as the psalmist grieves over the fact that many do not keep God's law. This verse challenges us to consider how we respond to the disobedience and spiritual lostness of those around us. Do we, like the psalmist, feel deep sorrow and compassion for those who do not follow God's law, and are we moved to pray for and encourage others to embrace His ways, or do we sometimes become indifferent or judgmental, failing to share the psalmist's passionate concern for the spiritual state of others?

As we explore the theme of dedication in Psalm 119, verses 129-136, we are reminded of the importance of renewing our commitment to God's precepts and cultivating a deep longing for others to follow His ways. The psalmist's example challenges us to consider how we approach our relationship with God's Word, especially in terms of our dedication to keeping His commands and our desire to see others embrace the truth and light of Scripture. Do we, like the psalmist, find God's testimonies so wonderful that our souls are naturally inclined to keep them, and do we long for the entrance of God's words to give light and understanding to all, or do we sometimes approach obedience as a burden, missing the beauty and majesty that the psalmist sees in God's commands?

Furthermore, the psalmist's intense longing for God's commandments, his recognition of the need for divine mercy, and his deep grief for those who do not follow God's law challenge us to deepen our own dedication to living according to Scripture. Are we willing to seek God's mercy and favor, asking Him to order our steps in His Word and deliver us from the oppression of others? Do we prioritize obedience to God's precepts even in the face of external pressures, and do we feel deep sorrow and compassion for those who do not follow His ways, praying for their hearts to be turned toward God?

In conclusion, the theme of dedication in Psalm 119, verses 129-136, offers a powerful reminder of the need to anchor our lives in a renewed commitment to God's precepts, while also cultivating a deep longing for others to follow His ways. The psalmist's unwavering commitment to God's commands, his intense desire for divine instruction and mercy, and his deep grief for those who do not keep God's law challenge us to deepen our own dedication to living according to Scripture. As we continue to explore the depths of Psalm 119, may we be inspired to reaffirm our commitment to God's Word, seeking the guidance and understanding that come from a life fully dedicated to His commandments, and recognizing that it is through our dedication to Scripture that we find the true purpose, guidance, and fulfillment we need to navigate the complexities and challenges of life.

Whether we are seeking to grow in our understanding of God's Word, striving to live a life that honors God, or feeling deep concern for the spiritual state of others, may we always turn to His Word as our source of guidance, instruction, and inspiration, knowing that it is through our dedication to His commandments that we find the true purpose and direction we need to live a life that is fully devoted to Him. The psalmist's example reminds us that true dedication is not just about keeping God's commands for ourselves, but also about longing to see others experience the light and truth of His Word. By placing our trust in God's Word and seeking His guidance in every aspect of our lives, we can experience the peace, strength, and fulfillment that come from living a life that is anchored in the truth of His commandments. As we continue to journey through Psalm 119, may we be encouraged to deepen our dedication to God's Word, finding in it the guidance, understanding, and inspiration we need to live a life that is fully devoted to Him, anchored in the truth of God's eternal Word.

Chapter 18 – The Divine Justice

In Psalm 119, verses 137-144, the theme of divine justice is deeply explored as the psalmist praises the righteousness of God's judgments and seeks understanding to live by His laws. These verses reflect the psalmist's profound reverence for God's inherent justice and the unwavering truth of His commandments, underscoring the importance of aligning one's life with the divine standards that God has established. The passage begins in verse 137 with a declaration of God's righteousness: "Righteous art thou, O Lord, and upright are thy judgments." This opening verse sets the tone for the entire passage, affirming the psalmist's belief that God's character is inherently righteous and that His judgments are completely just and upright. The use of "righteous" and "upright" emphasizes that God's decisions and decrees are not only correct but are also morally pure and fair, reflecting His perfect nature. This verse challenges us to consider how we view God's justice in our own lives. Do we, like the psalmist, acknowledge and praise God for His righteousness and uprightness, trusting that His judgments are always fair and just, even when we may not fully understand them, or do we sometimes question or doubt God's justice, especially in difficult circumstances?

In verse 138, the psalmist continues by acknowledging the faithfulness and truth of God's commandments: "Thy testimonies that thou hast commanded are righteous and very faithful." Here, the psalmist recognizes that not only are God's commandments righteous, but they are also "very faithful," meaning they are dependable and trustworthy. The phrase "that thou hast commanded" suggests that these testimonies come directly from God's authority, underscoring their divine origin and the psalmist's confidence in their reliability. This verse challenges us to reflect on our own trust in God's Word. Do we, like the psalmist, regard God's testimonies as not only righteous but also deeply faithful and trustworthy, or do we sometimes struggle to fully rely on the truth and dependability of God's commandments, especially when faced with conflicting messages from the world around us?

The psalmist's zeal for God's Word and his recognition of the opposition he faces is expressed in verse 139: "My zeal hath consumed me, because mine enemies have forgotten thy words." This verse reveals the intensity of the psalmist's dedication to God's commandments, to the point where his zeal—his passionate commitment—has "consumed" him. The use of the word "consumed" suggests that the psalmist is so deeply devoted to God's Word that it has become the driving force of his life, overwhelming him with a sense of purpose and urgency. The phrase "because mine enemies have forgotten thy words" highlights the psalmist's sorrow and frustration that others, particularly his enemies, have neglected or rejected the truth of God's commandments. This verse challenges us to consider the depth of our own commitment to God's Word. Do we, like the psalmist, feel a consuming zeal for God's commandments, motivated by the desire to see others uphold and remember His words, or do we sometimes lack the fervor and dedication needed to stand firm in our faith, especially when faced with opposition?

In verse 140, the psalmist expresses his deep love for God's Word, recognizing its purity: "Thy word is very pure: therefore thy servant loveth it." This verse highlights the psalmist's affection for God's Word, which he describes as "very pure," indicating that it is free from any corruption, error, or deceit. The purity of God's Word is what draws the psalmist's love, as he finds in it a source of truth and righteousness that is unmatched by anything else. The phrase "therefore thy servant loveth it" suggests that the psalmist's love for God's Word is a natural response to its purity and perfection. This verse challenges us to reflect on the nature of our own love for Scripture. Do we, like the psalmist, love God's Word because of its purity, recognizing that it is a flawless and trustworthy guide for our lives, or do we sometimes overlook the beauty and perfection of God's Word, failing to appreciate the depth of its truth?

The psalmist's acknowledgment of his own lowly state and his continued commitment to God's commandments is evident in verse 141: "I am small and despised: yet do not I forget thy precepts." This verse reveals the psalmist's humility and awareness of his own insignificance in the eyes of the world, as he describes himself as "small and despised." Despite this lowly status, the psalmist remains committed to God's precepts, refusing to forget or neglect them. The phrase "yet do not I forget thy precepts" indicates that the psalmist's dedication to God's Word is not dependent on his circumstances or how others perceive him, but is a steadfast commitment that endures even in the face of rejection or scorn. This verse challenges us to consider how we respond to feelings of insignificance or rejection. Do we, like the psalmist, remain faithful to God's precepts, regardless of how we are viewed by others or the challenges we face, or do we sometimes allow our circumstances or the opinions of others to shake our commitment to God's Word?

In verse 142, the psalmist reaffirms the eternal truth of God's righteousness and law: "Thy righteousness is an everlasting righteousness, and thy law is the truth." This verse emphasizes the eternal nature of God's righteousness, which is not subject to change or decay over time. The phrase "an everlasting righteousness" suggests that God's justice and moral standards are timeless, enduring forever without alteration. The psalmist also declares that "thy law is the truth," affirming that God's commandments are the ultimate standard of truth, providing a foundation upon which all other truths must be measured. This verse challenges us to reflect on our own understanding of truth and righteousness. Do we, like the psalmist, recognize that God's righteousness is everlasting and that His law is the ultimate truth, or do we sometimes allow ourselves to be swayed by the shifting values and standards of the world, forgetting the eternal nature of God's Word?

The psalmist's expression of distress and his reliance on God's commandments for comfort is expressed in verse 143: "Trouble and anguish have taken hold on me: yet thy commandments are my delights." This verse reveals the psalmist's experience of deep emotional and spiritual distress, as he describes being gripped by "trouble and anguish." Despite these overwhelming feelings, the psalmist finds solace and joy in God's commandments, which he describes as "my delights." The phrase "yet thy commandments are my delights" indicates that the psalmist's love for God's Word is so strong that it brings him comfort and joy even in the midst of his greatest trials. This verse challenges us to consider where we find comfort in times of distress. Do we, like the psalmist, turn to God's commandments as a source of delight and solace when we are troubled and anguished, or do we sometimes seek comfort in other, less reliable sources, neglecting the peace and joy that come from living according to God's Word?

The passage concludes in verse 144 with a final affirmation of the righteousness of God's testimonies and a plea for understanding: "The righteousness of thy testimonies is everlasting: give me understanding, and I shall live." This verse echoes the themes of earlier verses, emphasizing the eternal nature of God's righteousness and the enduring truth of His testimonies. The psalmist's plea for understanding reflects his recognition that true life—both physical and spiritual—comes from living in accordance with God's Word. The phrase "give me understanding, and I shall live" suggests that the psalmist sees the knowledge and application of God's Word as essential to his survival and well-being. This verse challenges us to reflect on our own pursuit of understanding and how it relates to our spiritual vitality. Do we, like the psalmist, recognize that true life is found in understanding and living by God's testimonies, and do we actively seek the wisdom and insight that come from Scripture, or do we sometimes neglect the importance of understanding God's Word, missing out on the fullness of life that it offers?

As we explore the theme of divine justice in Psalm 119, verses 137-144, we are reminded of the importance of praising God for the righteousness of His judgments and seeking understanding to live by His laws. The psalmist's example challenges us to consider how we approach God's justice and truth in our own lives, especially in terms of our dedication to His commandments and our desire for understanding. Do we, like the psalmist, acknowledge and praise God for His righteousness and uprightness, trusting that His judgments are always fair and just, and do we seek the understanding that comes from living according to His Word, or do we sometimes struggle to fully trust in God's justice and righteousness, especially when faced with difficult or confusing circumstances?

Furthermore, the psalmist's expression of zeal for God's Word, his recognition of its purity and truth, and his reliance on God's commandments for comfort and guidance challenge us to deepen our own commitment to living according to Scripture. Are we willing to embrace the purity and truth of God's Word, allowing it to guide our lives and bring us comfort in times of distress? Do we value God's commandments above all else, recognizing their eternal righteousness and truth, and do we actively seek the understanding that comes from living according to His testimonies, knowing that this is the key to true life and fulfillment?

In conclusion, the theme of divine justice in Psalm 119, verses 137-144, offers a powerful reminder of the need to anchor our lives in the righteousness and truth of God's Word, especially when seeking understanding and guidance in a world

that is often marked by injustice and confusion. The psalmist's unwavering commitment to praising God's judgments, his deep love for the purity and truth of God's Word, and his plea for understanding challenge us to deepen our own dedication to living according to Scripture. As we continue to explore the depths of Psalm 119, may we be inspired to reaffirm our commitment to God's Word, seeking the understanding and guidance that come from a life fully dedicated to His commandments, and recognizing that it is through our dedication to Scripture that we find the true purpose, guidance, and fulfillment we need to navigate the complexities and challenges of life.

Whether we are seeking to grow in our understanding of God's Word, striving to live a life that honors God, or feeling the weight of trouble and anguish, may we always turn to His Word as our source of truth, righteousness, and inspiration, knowing that it is through our dedication to His commandments that we find the true purpose and direction we need to live a life that is fully devoted to Him. The psalmist's example reminds us that true justice and understanding are not found in human wisdom or in the shifting standards of the world, but in the eternal and unchanging truth of God's Word. By placing our trust in God's Word and seeking His understanding in every aspect of our lives, we can experience the peace, strength, and fulfillment that come from living a life that is anchored in the truth of His commandments. As we continue to journey through Psalm 119, may we be encouraged to deepen our commitment to seeking divine justice and understanding through God's Word, finding in it the strength, guidance, and inspiration we need to live a life that is fully devoted to Him, anchored in the truth of God's eternal Word.

Chapter 19 – The Dependence

In Psalm 119, verses 145-152, the theme of dependence is profoundly expressed as the psalmist reveals his deep reliance on God's commandments and promises, especially during times of urgent need. These verses encapsulate the psalmist's intense trust in God's Word as his lifeline, the source of strength, guidance, and hope in moments of desperation. The passage begins in verse 145 with a heartfelt cry for help: "I cried with my whole heart; hear me, O Lord: I will keep thy statutes." This opening verse sets the tone for the psalmist's plea, highlighting his complete and undivided dependence on God. The phrase "I cried with my whole heart" signifies the intensity and sincerity of the psalmist's prayer, emphasizing that his entire being is engaged in seeking God's help. This deep cry is not just a casual request but a desperate appeal, demonstrating that the psalmist's trust in God's statutes is absolute. The commitment to "keep thy statutes" even in such distress reflects the psalmist's unwavering dedication to God's commandments, showing that his dependence on God is rooted in a deep commitment to obedience. This verse challenges us to consider how we respond when we face urgent needs or crises in our own lives. Do we, like the psalmist, cry out to God with our whole heart, fully depending on His Word and committing ourselves to keep His statutes, or do we sometimes seek other sources of help, forgetting the strength and guidance that come from God's promises?

In verse 146, the psalmist continues his plea for deliverance: "I cried unto thee; save me, and I shall keep thy testimonies." This verse reinforces the urgency of the psalmist's situation, as he repeats his cry for help, specifically asking for salvation. The phrase "I cried unto thee" underscores the psalmist's recognition that only God can deliver him from his distress. The request "save me" is simple yet profound, capturing the essence of the psalmist's reliance on God's power to rescue him. The commitment to "keep thy testimonies" even in the midst of seeking salvation highlights the psalmist's determination to remain faithful to God's Word, no matter the circumstances. This verse challenges us to reflect on our own dependence on God's deliverance. Do we, like the psalmist, turn to God first in our times of need, crying out for His salvation and promising to keep His testimonies as a response to His deliverance, or do we sometimes waver in our faith, unsure of where to turn or what promises to hold onto?

The psalmist's early morning devotion and dependence on God's Word are vividly portrayed in verse 147: "I prevented the dawning of the morning, and cried: I hoped in thy word." This verse reveals the psalmist's deep commitment to seeking God, even before the break of day. The phrase "I prevented the dawning of the morning" suggests that the psalmist rises early, even before the sun, to cry out to God, indicating that his dependence on God is so great that it cannot wait until later in the day. The act of crying out in the early morning hours reflects the psalmist's eagerness to connect with God, showing that his hope is firmly placed in God's Word. This verse challenges us to consider the priority we give to seeking God in our own lives. Do we, like the psalmist, rise early and eagerly seek God's presence and guidance, placing our hope in His Word above all else, or do we sometimes delay or neglect our time with God, allowing other concerns to take precedence over our dependence on His promises?

In verse 148, the psalmist further emphasizes his dedication to God's Word: "Mine eyes prevent the night watches, that I might meditate in thy word." This verse complements the previous one by showing that the psalmist's devotion to God's Word extends not only to the early morning but also to the late night hours. The phrase "prevent the night watches" suggests that the psalmist stays awake during the night, meditating on God's Word instead of sleeping. This level of commitment indicates that the psalmist finds solace, strength, and guidance in Scripture, even when others might be resting. The act of meditating on God's Word during the night watches reflects the psalmist's deep dependence on Scripture as the foundation of his life. This verse challenges us to examine our own dedication to meditating on God's Word. Do we, like the psalmist, prioritize spending time in Scripture, even during the night, recognizing its importance for our spiritual well-being, or do we sometimes allow the busyness of life or the need for rest to overshadow our commitment to meditating on God's Word?

The psalmist's appeal to God's loving-kindness is expressed in verse 149: "Hear my voice according unto thy lovingkindness: O Lord, quicken me according to thy judgment." This verse reveals the psalmist's understanding that God's response to his cries is rooted in divine loving-kindness, a term that conveys God's steadfast love, mercy, and compassion. The phrase "according unto thy lovingkindness" indicates that the psalmist's hope for deliverance is based not on his own merit but on God's gracious character. The request to be "quickened" or revived according to God's judgment reflects the psalmist's desire for spiritual renewal and life, recognizing that true revival comes from aligning oneself with God's righteous judgments. This verse challenges us to consider how we approach God in prayer, especially when seeking revival or deliverance. Do we, like the psalmist, appeal to God's loving-kindness and seek to be quickened according to His judgment, trusting in His mercy and righteousness, or do we sometimes rely on our own efforts or understanding, forgetting that true life and renewal come from God's gracious and just nature?

In verse 150, the psalmist acknowledges the nearness of those who oppose him: "They draw nigh that follow after mischief: they are far from thy law." This verse reveals the psalmist's awareness of the imminent threat posed by those who pursue "mischief" or evil, and who are "far from thy law." The contrast between the nearness of the wicked and their distance from God's law highlights the psalmist's understanding of the spiritual danger they represent. Despite their proximity, the psalmist remains focused on God's Word, implying that his dependence on God's commandments provides him with the strength and guidance needed to face these adversaries. This verse challenges us to reflect on how we respond to the presence of those who oppose us or reject God's law. Do we, like the psalmist, remain steadfast in our dependence on God's Word, trusting in its guidance and protection even when we are surrounded by those who pursue mischief, or do we sometimes feel overwhelmed or discouraged by the opposition we face, losing sight of the strength and direction that come from Scripture?

The psalmist's assurance of God's nearness and faithfulness is beautifully expressed in verse 151: "Thou art near, O Lord; and all thy commandments are truth." This verse contrasts the nearness of the wicked in the previous verse with the comforting nearness of the Lord. The phrase "Thou art near, O Lord" reflects the psalmist's confidence in God's presence, even in the midst of adversity. The declaration that "all thy commandments are truth" underscores the psalmist's belief that God's Word is completely reliable and trustworthy, providing a firm foundation for his life. This verse challenges us to consider our own sense of God's presence in our lives. Do we, like the psalmist, experience the nearness of the Lord, trusting in the truth of His commandments as our anchor in times of trouble, or do we sometimes struggle to feel God's presence, especially when facing difficulties or challenges?

The passage concludes in verse 152 with a reflection on the enduring nature of God's Word: "Concerning thy testimonies, I have known of old that thou hast founded them for ever." This final verse reveals the psalmist's deep conviction that God's testimonies are eternal, having been "founded for ever." The phrase "I have known of old" suggests that the psalmist's faith in the enduring nature of God's Word is based on long-standing experience and understanding. This acknowledgment of the eternal foundation of God's testimonies provides the psalmist with confidence and assurance, knowing that the Word of God will never change or fail. This verse challenges us to reflect on our own understanding of the permanence and reliability of God's Word. Do we, like the psalmist, recognize that God's testimonies are founded forever, providing a stable and unchanging foundation for our lives, or do we sometimes forget the eternal nature of God's Word, allowing temporary circumstances to shake our faith and dependence on His promises?

As we explore the theme of dependence in Psalm 119, verses 145-152, we are reminded of the importance of relying on God's commandments and promises, especially in times of urgent need. The psalmist's example challenges us to consider how we respond to crises and difficulties in our own lives, particularly in terms of our reliance on God's Word and our commitment to obedience. Do we, like the psalmist, cry out to God with our whole heart, fully depending on His Word and committing ourselves to keep His statutes, even in the midst of distress? Do we seek God's deliverance with the confidence that His loving-kindness and righteous judgment will revive and sustain us, or do we sometimes struggle to fully trust in God's promises, feeling overwhelmed by the challenges we face?

Furthermore, the psalmist's early morning and late-night devotion to God's Word, his appeal to God's loving-kindness, and his assurance of God's nearness challenge us to deepen our own commitment to living according to Scripture. Are we willing to prioritize seeking God's presence and guidance, even in the early hours of the morning or the stillness of the night? Do we trust in God's loving-kindness and righteous judgment to revive and deliver us, and do we remain confident in the nearness and truth of the Lord, even when surrounded by those who oppose His law?

In conclusion, the theme of dependence in Psalm 119, verses 145-152, offers a powerful reminder of the need to anchor our lives in the commandments and promises of God, especially during times of urgent need. The psalmist's unwavering trust in God's Word, his deep commitment to seeking God's presence and guidance, and his assurance of the eternal foundation of God's testimonies challenge us to deepen our own dependence on Scripture. As we continue to explore the depths of Psalm 119, may we be inspired to reaffirm our commitment to God's Word, seeking the strength, guidance, and hope that come from a life fully dependent on His commandments, and recognizing that it is through our reliance on Scripture that we find the true purpose, guidance, and fulfillment we need to navigate the complexities and challenges of life.

Whether we are seeking to grow in our understanding of God's Word, striving to live a life that honors God, or facing moments of urgent need and distress, may we always turn to His Word as our source of strength, guidance, and inspiration, knowing that it is through our dependence on His commandments that we find the true purpose and direction we need to live a life that is fully devoted to Him. The psalmist's example reminds us that true dependence is not found in human strength or in the shifting circumstances of the world, but in the eternal and unchanging truth of God's Word. By placing our trust in God's Word and seeking His guidance in every aspect of our lives, we can experience the peace, strength, and fulfillment that come from living a life that is anchored in the truth of His commandments. As we continue to journey through Psalm 119, may we be encouraged to deepen our commitment to seeking dependence on God's Word, finding in it the strength, guidance, and inspiration we need to live a life that is fully devoted to Him, anchored in the truth of God's eternal Word.

Chapter 20 – The Devotion

In Psalm 119, verses 153-160, the theme of devotion is profoundly explored as the psalmist pleads for God's attention and intervention, emphasizing that his unwavering devotion to God's Word is the foundation of his life. These verses encapsulate the psalmist's deep commitment to living according to God's commandments, even in the face of adversity and distress, while also expressing his urgent need for God's deliverance and vindication. The passage begins in verse 153 with a heartfelt cry for God's awareness and action: "Consider mine affliction, and deliver me: for I do not forget thy law." This opening verse sets the tone for the psalmist's plea, highlighting his reliance on God's attention to his suffering and his expectation of divine intervention. The word "consider" suggests that the psalmist is asking God to take notice of his situation, to see the depth of his affliction and respond with deliverance. The phrase "for I do not forget thy law" indicates that the psalmist's devotion to God's commandments is unwavering, even in the midst of his trials, and it is this steadfast adherence to God's law that forms the basis of his plea for deliverance. This verse challenges us to consider how we respond when we face affliction in our own lives. Do we, like the psalmist, call out to God with the confidence that He sees our struggles and will deliver us, basing our plea on our devotion to His Word, or do we sometimes falter in our faith, forgetting to rely on the strength and guidance that come from Scripture?

In verse 154, the psalmist continues his plea, asking for divine advocacy and life: "Plead my cause, and deliver me: quicken me according to thy word." This verse emphasizes the psalmist's desire for God to act as his advocate, to "plead my cause," suggesting that he sees God as the ultimate judge who can vindicate him and deliver him from his troubles. The request to "quicken me according to thy word" reflects the psalmist's recognition that true life and vitality come from God's Word. The term "quicken" means to revive or bring to life, indicating that the psalmist is seeking not just physical deliverance but also spiritual renewal, grounded in the promises and truths of Scripture. This verse challenges us to reflect on where we seek advocacy and life in our own times of trouble. Do we, like the psalmist, turn to

God as our ultimate advocate, asking Him to plead our cause and revive us according to His Word, or do we sometimes look to other sources for vindication and renewal, forgetting that true life comes from God alone?

The psalmist's acknowledgment of the presence of wickedness and the absence of true salvation apart from God is expressed in verse 155: "Salvation is far from the wicked: for they seek not thy statutes." This verse highlights the psalmist's understanding that those who reject God's statutes are distant from true salvation, which can only be found in obedience to God's Word. The phrase "salvation is far from the wicked" reflects the psalmist's recognition that without a commitment to God's commandments, deliverance and redemption are out of reach. This understanding further emphasizes the psalmist's devotion to God's Word as the basis for life and salvation. This verse challenges us to consider how we view the relationship between obedience to God's Word and the experience of salvation. Do we, like the psalmist, recognize that true salvation is intimately connected to seeking and following God's statutes, or do we sometimes overlook the importance of living in accordance with Scripture, assuming that salvation can be attained without a commitment to God's commands?

In verse 156, the psalmist expresses his deep trust in God's mercy and his plea for life according to God's judgments: "Great are thy tender mercies, O Lord: quicken me according to thy judgments." This verse reveals the psalmist's reliance on God's compassionate and loving nature, described here as "tender mercies." The acknowledgment of the greatness of God's mercies suggests that the psalmist is deeply aware of God's kindness and willingness to forgive and restore. The request to be "quickened" or revived according to God's judgments reflects the psalmist's desire for his life to be aligned with God's righteous decisions, understanding that true life is found in living according to God's will. This verse challenges us to consider how we approach God's mercy and judgments in our own lives. Do we, like the psalmist, trust in the greatness of God's tender mercies and seek to be revived according to His judgments, recognizing that true life comes from living in harmony with God's righteous decisions, or do we sometimes take God's mercy for granted, failing to align our lives with His will?

The psalmist's frustration with the faithlessness of his enemies is vividly portrayed in verse 157: "Many are my persecutors and mine enemies; yet do I not decline from thy testimonies." This verse highlights the psalmist's steadfast devotion to God's Word, even in the face of numerous adversaries who seek to persecute and harm him. The phrase "yet do I not decline from thy testimonies" indicates that despite the overwhelming opposition, the psalmist remains committed to following God's commandments. This unwavering dedication demonstrates the psalmist's belief that God's testimonies are the foundation of his life, and no amount of persecution can cause him to turn away from them. This verse challenges us to reflect on how we respond to opposition and persecution in our own lives. Do we, like the psalmist, remain steadfast in our devotion to God's Word, refusing to decline from His testimonies even when faced with many adversaries, or do we sometimes allow the pressures and challenges of life to weaken our commitment to living according to Scripture?

In verse 158, the psalmist expresses his grief over the disobedience of others: "I beheld the transgressors, and was grieved; because they kept not thy word." This verse reveals the psalmist's deep sorrow and frustration as he observes those who transgress or violate God's law. The phrase "I beheld the transgressors" suggests that the psalmist has seen firsthand the actions of those who reject God's commandments, and this sight causes him great grief. The reason for his grief is clear: "because they kept not thy word." The psalmist's devotion to God's Word is so strong that the disobedience of others brings him genuine sorrow, highlighting his deep concern for the spiritual state of those who have turned away from God's commands. This verse challenges us to consider how we react to the disobedience of others. Do we, like the psalmist, feel genuine grief and concern when we see others transgressing God's law, motivated by a deep devotion to His Word and a desire for others to live according to His commandments, or do we sometimes respond with indifference or judgment, failing to share the psalmist's compassionate concern?

The psalmist's unwavering love for God's precepts and his commitment to living by them are expressed in verse 159: "Consider how I love thy precepts: quicken me, O Lord, according to thy lovingkindness." This verse reveals the psalmist's deep affection for God's precepts, which he asks God to "consider," or take into account. The phrase "how I love thy precepts" reflects the psalmist's passionate devotion to God's Word, indicating that his love for God's commandments is a central aspect of his life. The request to be "quickened" or revived according to God's lovingkindness emphasizes the psalmist's reliance on God's compassionate nature to bring him life and vitality, rooted in his devotion to God's precepts. This verse challenges us to reflect on the depth of our own love for God's Word. Do we, like the psalmist, have a deep and abiding love for God's precepts, and do we seek to be revived and sustained by His lovingkindness, recognizing that true life is found in a devoted relationship with His Word, or do we sometimes neglect or take for granted the importance of living according to God's commands?

The passage concludes in verse 160 with a powerful affirmation of the truth and enduring nature of God's Word: "Thy word is true from the beginning: and every one of thy righteous judgments endureth for ever." This final verse encapsulates the psalmist's unwavering belief in the absolute truth and eternal nature of God's Word. The phrase "thy word is true from the beginning" suggests that the psalmist recognizes the consistency and reliability of God's Word throughout all time, from the very beginning of creation. The declaration that "every one of thy righteous judgments endureth for ever" emphasizes the eternal nature of God's decisions and commandments, highlighting that they are unchanging and will stand forever. This verse challenges us to reflect on our own understanding of the truth and permanence of God's Word. Do we, like the psalmist, recognize that God's Word is true from the beginning and that His righteous judgments endure forever, providing a firm and unshakable foundation for our lives, or do we sometimes allow the transient nature of the world around us to influence our perception of God's truth?

As we explore the theme of devotion in Psalm 119, verses 153-160, we are reminded of the importance of pleading for God's attention and intervention, with a deep and unwavering devotion to His Word as the basis for life. The psalmist's example challenges us to consider how we approach our relationship with God's Word, especially in terms of our dedication to living according to His commandments and our reliance on His promises in times of need. Do we recognize the eternal truth of God's Word and the enduring nature of His righteous judgments, allowing them to guide our lives and provide a firm foundation in a world that is constantly changing?

In conclusion, the theme of devotion in Psalm 119, verses 153-160, offers a powerful reminder of the need to anchor our lives in a deep and unwavering commitment to God's Word, especially when seeking His attention and intervention in times of need. The psalmist's unwavering trust in God's mercy and righteousness, his deep commitment to seeking God's presence and guidance, and his assurance of the eternal foundation of God's testimonies challenge us to deepen our own devotion to Scripture. As we continue to explore the depths of Psalm 119, may we be inspired to reaffirm our commitment to God's Word, seeking the strength, guidance, and hope that come from a life fully devoted to His commandments, and recognizing that it is through our devotion to Scripture that we find the true purpose, guidance, and fulfillment we need to navigate the complexities and challenges of life.

Whether we are seeking to grow in our understanding of God's Word, striving to live a life that honors God, or facing moments of urgent need and distress, may we always turn to His Word as our source of strength, guidance, and inspiration, knowing that it is through our devotion to His commandments that we find the true purpose and direction we need to live a life that is fully devoted to Him. The psalmist's example reminds us that true devotion is not found in half-hearted commitment or in the shifting circumstances of the world, but in the eternal and unchanging truth of God's Word. By placing our trust in God's Word and seeking His guidance in every aspect of our lives, we can experience the peace, strength, and fulfillment that come from living a life that is anchored in the truth of His commandments. As we continue to journey through Psalm 119, may we be encouraged to deepen our commitment to seeking devotion to God's Word, finding in it the strength, guidance, and inspiration we need to live a life that is fully devoted to Him, anchored in the truth of God's eternal Word.

Chapter 21 – The Deliverance

In Psalm 119, verses 161-168, the theme of deliverance is intricately woven into the psalmist's plea for relief from persecution, all while expressing a profound sense of peace and joy found in God's commandments. These verses capture the psalmist's deep trust in God's Word as both his refuge and source of deliverance, highlighting the contrast between the external pressures of persecution and the internal tranquility derived from steadfast obedience to God's law. The passage begins in verse 161 with a declaration of the intensity of the psalmist's trials: "Princes have persecuted me without a cause: but my heart standeth in awe of thy word." This opening verse sets the tone for the psalmist's experience, where he acknowledges the unjust persecution he faces from those in power—"princes" who pursue him "without a cause." Despite this unjust treatment, the psalmist's response is not one of despair or anger; instead, his heart remains firmly anchored in reverence and awe for God's Word. The phrase "my heart standeth in awe of thy word" suggests that the psalmist finds solace and strength in Scripture, which enables him to endure persecution with a calm and unwavering spirit. This verse challenges us to consider how we respond to unjust treatment or persecution in our own lives. Do we, like the psalmist, maintain a deep reverence and awe for God's Word, allowing it to be our anchor in times of trouble, or do we sometimes let the pressures of external circumstances shake our faith and erode our sense of peace?

In verse 162, the psalmist continues by expressing the joy he finds in God's Word: "I rejoice at thy word, as one that findeth great spoil." This verse vividly illustrates the psalmist's delight in God's commandments, comparing it to the joy of discovering "great spoil" or treasure. The metaphor of finding treasure emphasizes the immense value the psalmist places on Scripture, viewing it as a priceless gift that brings joy and fulfillment. This rejoicing in God's Word, even in the midst of persecution, reveals the psalmist's deep conviction that the true riches of life are found in the wisdom and guidance of Scripture, rather than in material wealth or worldly success. This verse challenges us to reflect on the source of our own joy and fulfillment. Do we, like the psalmist, rejoice in God's Word as a treasure beyond compare, finding in it the source of true happiness and peace, or do we sometimes seek joy in other, less lasting things, neglecting the richness and depth that come from immersing ourselves in Scripture?

The psalmist's commitment to integrity and truth is highlighted in verse 163: "I hate and abhor lying: but thy law do I love." This verse contrasts the psalmist's strong aversion to falsehood with his deep love for God's law. The use of the words "hate" and "abhor" underscores the intensity of the psalmist's rejection of deceit and dishonesty, indicating that he sees lying as completely incompatible with the truth of God's commandments. The phrase "but thy law do I love" suggests that the psalmist's love for God's law is what drives his commitment to truth and integrity, providing him with a moral compass that guides his actions and decisions. This verse challenges us to examine our own attitudes toward truth and honesty. Do we, like the psalmist, abhor lying and cling to the truth of God's law, allowing it to shape our character and conduct, or do we sometimes compromise our integrity, forgetting the importance of living in accordance with the truth of Scripture?

In verse 164, the psalmist expresses his devotion to praising God throughout the day: "Seven times a day do I praise thee because of thy righteous judgments." This verse reveals the psalmist's disciplined and frequent practice of worship, as he praises God "seven times a day" in response to the righteousness of God's judgments. The number seven, often associated with completeness and perfection in the Bible, suggests that the psalmist's praise is not occasional or sporadic, but a regular and intentional part of his daily life. The phrase "because of thy righteous judgments" indicates that the psalmist's praise is rooted in his recognition of God's perfect justice and the rightness of His decisions, which further deepens his trust and joy in God's Word. This verse challenges us to consider how we incorporate praise and worship into our daily routines. Do we, like the psalmist, make a regular practice of praising God throughout the day, acknowledging His righteousness and justice in all circumstances, or do we sometimes neglect to express our gratitude and reverence for God's judgments, allowing the busyness of life to crowd out our worship?

The psalmist's experience of peace and security is powerfully expressed in verse 165: "Great peace have they which love thy law: and nothing shall offend them." This verse highlights the profound sense of peace that comes from loving and living according to God's law. The phrase "great peace" suggests that the peace experienced by those who love God's law is not just a temporary feeling, but a deep and abiding sense of well-being and contentment. The statement "nothing shall offend them" indicates that those who are anchored in God's Word are not easily shaken or disturbed by external circumstances, including persecution or adversity. This verse challenges us to reflect on the source of our own peace and security. Do we, like the psalmist, find great peace in loving God's law, trusting that nothing can offend or disturb us when we are firmly rooted in Scripture, or do we sometimes allow external challenges or conflicts to disrupt our inner peace, forgetting the stability and security that come from living according to God's Word?

In verse 166, the psalmist expresses his hope for God's salvation, grounded in his obedience to God's commandments: "Lord, I have hoped for thy salvation, and done thy commandments." This verse reveals the psalmist's confident expectation of deliverance, based on his faithful adherence to God's commandments. The phrase "I have hoped for thy salvation" indicates that the psalmist's trust in God's deliverance is not passive, but active and hopeful, rooted in the conviction that God's promises will be fulfilled. The statement "and done thy commandments" suggests that the psalmist's hope is accompanied by a commitment to living in obedience to God's Word, recognizing that true salvation is found in aligning one's life with God's will. This verse challenges us to consider how we approach the concept of salvation in our own lives. Do we, like the psalmist, place our hope in God's salvation while actively living according to His commandments, trusting that our obedience and faithfulness will lead to deliverance, or do we sometimes separate our hope for salvation from our daily actions, neglecting the importance of living in accordance with God's Word?

The psalmist's dedication to observing God's precepts with love is further emphasized in verse 167: "My soul hath kept thy testimonies; and I love them exceedingly." This verse reflects the psalmist's deep and personal commitment to keeping God's testimonies, which he loves "exceedingly." The use of the word "soul" suggests that the psalmist's devotion is not merely external or superficial, but is rooted in the very core of his being. The phrase "I love them exceedingly" indicates that the psalmist's love for God's testimonies is intense and wholehearted, driving his commitment to living according to God's Word. This verse challenges us to reflect on the depth of our own love for God's Word. Do we, like the psalmist, keep God's testimonies with our whole soul, loving them exceedingly and allowing them to shape every aspect of our lives, or do we sometimes struggle to maintain such a deep and consistent devotion, letting other priorities or distractions take precedence?

The passage concludes in verse 168 with a declaration of the psalmist's observance of God's precepts and the transparency of his life before God: "I have kept thy precepts and thy testimonies: for all my ways are before thee." This final verse encapsulates the psalmist's unwavering commitment to living according to God's precepts and testimonies, with the acknowledgment that all his ways are fully known to God. The phrase "all my ways are before thee" suggests that the psalmist lives with the awareness that God sees and knows everything about him, and this awareness reinforces his commitment to obedience and integrity. This verse challenges us to consider how we live our lives in relation to God's omniscience. Do we, like the psalmist, live with the understanding that all our ways are before God, striving to keep His precepts and testimonies with integrity and transparency, or do we sometimes forget that God sees and knows everything about us, leading to lapses in our commitment to living according to His Word?

As we explore the theme of deliverance in Psalm 119, verses 161-168, we are reminded of the importance of seeking God's deliverance from persecution while finding peace and joy in His commandments. The psalmist's example challenges us to consider how we respond to trials and adversity in our own lives, particularly in terms of our reliance on God's Word and our commitment to obedience. Do we, like the psalmist, maintain a deep reverence and awe for God's Word, rejoicing in its truth and finding great peace in our love for His law, even when faced with unjust treatment or persecution? Do we seek God's deliverance with the confidence that His righteous judgments will prevail, and do we live with the awareness that all our ways are before Him, striving to keep His precepts with integrity and devotion?

Furthermore, the psalmist's disciplined practice of praise, his deep love for God's law, and his recognition of the peace that comes from living according to God's commandments challenge us to deepen our own commitment to living according to Scripture. Are we willing to make praise and worship a regular part of our daily lives, acknowledging God's righteousness and justice in all circumstances? Do we recognize that true peace and security are found in loving God's law and living in accordance with His Word, and do we strive to keep His precepts with our whole soul, loving them exceedingly and allowing them to guide every aspect of our lives?

In conclusion, the theme of deliverance in Psalm 119, verses 161-168, offers a powerful reminder of the need to anchor our lives in the peace and joy that come from loving and living according to

God's commandments, especially when seeking His deliverance from persecution and adversity. The psalmist's unwavering trust in God's Word, his deep commitment to praising God's righteous judgments, and his assurance of the peace that comes from loving God's law challenge us to deepen our own dependence on Scripture. As we continue to explore the depths of Psalm 119, may we be inspired to reaffirm our commitment to God's Word, seeking the strength, guidance, and peace that come from a life fully devoted to His commandments, and recognizing that it is through our love for and obedience to Scripture that we find the true purpose, guidance, and fulfillment we need to navigate the complexities and challenges of life.

Whether we are seeking to grow in our understanding of God's Word, striving to live a life that honors God, or facing moments of persecution and adversity, may we always turn to His Word as our source of strength, guidance, and inspiration, knowing that it is through our love for His commandments that we find the true peace and deliverance we need to live a life that is fully devoted to Him. The psalmist's example reminds us that true deliverance and peace are not found in human strength or in the changing circumstances of the world, but in the eternal and unchanging truth of God's Word. By placing our trust in God's Word and seeking His guidance in every aspect of our lives, we can experience the peace, strength, and fulfillment that come from living a life that is anchored in the truth of His commandments. As we continue to journey through Psalm 119, may we be encouraged to deepen our commitment to seeking deliverance through God's Word, finding in it the strength, guidance, and inspiration we need to live a life that is fully devoted to Him, anchored in the truth of God's eternal Word.

Chapter 22 – The Doxology

In Psalm 119, verses 169-176, the theme of doxology—an expression of praise to God—is woven into the psalmist's final words, where he offers heartfelt praise, requests understanding, and reaffirms his deep commitment to God's Word while acknowledging his profound need for God's guidance, likening himself to a lost sheep. These concluding verses serve as a powerful summation of the psalmist's spiritual journey, capturing his unwavering devotion to God's commandments and his deep sense of dependence on divine direction and mercy. The passage begins in verse 169 with a fervent plea: "Let my cry come near before thee, O Lord: give me understanding according to thy word." This opening verse sets the tone for the psalmist's closing prayer, where he seeks God's attention and asks for the gift of understanding. The phrase "let my cry come near before thee" reflects the psalmist's earnest desire for God to hear his prayer, emphasizing the closeness and intimacy he seeks with the Divine. The request for understanding "according to thy word" underscores the psalmist's recognition that true wisdom and insight can only come from aligning his thoughts and actions with the teachings of Scripture. This verse challenges us to consider how we approach God in our own prayers. Do we, like the psalmist, cry out to God with a sincere desire for understanding, recognizing that true wisdom is found in His Word, or do we sometimes seek answers and direction apart from Scripture, relying on our own limited understanding?

In verse 170, the psalmist continues his plea, asking for deliverance: "Let my supplication come before thee: deliver me according to thy word." This verse echoes the psalmist's earlier requests for God's intervention, highlighting his reliance on divine deliverance. The word "supplication" indicates a humble and earnest request, showing that the psalmist approaches God with a spirit of humility and dependence. The phrase "deliver me according to thy word" reveals the psalmist's deep trust in the promises of Scripture, believing that God's Word is the ultimate source of deliverance and salvation. This verse challenges us to reflect on our own prayers for deliverance. Do we, like the psalmist, approach God with humility and trust, asking for deliverance in accordance with His Word, or do we sometimes approach God with a sense of entitlement or impatience, forgetting the importance of aligning our requests with His promises?

The psalmist's expression of praise is vividly portrayed in verse 171: "My lips shall utter praise, when thou hast taught me thy statutes." This verse reveals the psalmist's commitment to praising God, particularly in response to the instruction and understanding he receives from God's Word. The phrase "my lips shall utter praise" suggests that the psalmist's praise is not a one-time event but a continuous and natural outpouring of gratitude and reverence. The condition "when thou hast taught me thy statutes" indicates that the psalmist's praise is directly tied to his learning and understanding of God's commandments, showing that he values the wisdom and guidance that come from Scripture. This verse challenges us to consider how we respond to the teaching and instruction we receive from God's Word. Do we, like the psalmist, offer continuous praise to God as we grow in our understanding of His statutes, recognizing that learning from Scripture is a gift worthy of celebration, or do we sometimes take our spiritual education for granted, neglecting to express our gratitude for the insights and guidance we receive?

In verse 172, the psalmist further emphasizes the connection between praise and God's Word: "My tongue shall speak of thy word: for all thy commandments are righteousness." This verse highlights the psalmist's dedication to proclaiming the truths of God's Word, using his "tongue" as an instrument of testimony and praise. The phrase "shall speak of thy word" indicates that the psalmist is committed to sharing the teachings of Scripture with others, recognizing the importance of verbalizing his faith and devotion. The reason for this proclamation is clear: "for all thy commandments are righteousness." The psalmist acknowledges that God's commandments are the embodiment of righteousness, providing a moral and ethical foundation for life. This verse challenges us to reflect on how we use our own voices to speak of God's Word. Do we, like the psalmist, make a habit of speaking about Scripture, sharing its truths and insights with others, and recognizing that God's commandments are the ultimate standard of righteousness, or do we sometimes remain silent about our faith, missing opportunities to proclaim the goodness and truth of God's Word?

The psalmist's request for help is expressed in verse 173: "Let thine hand help me; for I have chosen thy precepts." This verse reveals the psalmist's acknowledgment of his need for God's assistance, coupled with a declaration of his intentional choice to follow God's commandments. The phrase "let thine hand help me" reflects the psalmist's dependence on God's strength and guidance, recognizing that he cannot navigate life's challenges on his own. The statement "for I have chosen thy precepts" indicates that the psalmist's plea for help is rooted in his commitment to living according to God's Word, suggesting that he sees his obedience as the foundation for receiving God's support. This verse challenges us to consider how we seek God's help in our own lives. Do we, like the psalmist, acknowledge our need for divine assistance and base our requests for help on our commitment to following God's precepts, or do we sometimes seek God's help without considering our own responsibility to live in accordance with His Word?

In verse 174, the psalmist expresses his longing for God's salvation and his delight in God's law: "I have longed for thy salvation, O Lord; and thy law is my delight." This verse captures the psalmist's deep yearning for deliverance, coupled with his genuine joy in God's law. The phrase "I have longed for thy salvation" indicates that the psalmist's desire for deliverance is intense and enduring, reflecting his trust in God's ability to save. The statement "and thy law is my delight" suggests that even as the psalmist waits for salvation, he finds great pleasure and satisfaction in living according to God's commandments. This verse challenges us to reflect on our own attitudes toward salvation and obedience. Do we, like the psalmist, long for God's salvation with deep yearning while simultaneously finding delight in His law, recognizing that obedience to God's Word brings joy and fulfillment, or do we sometimes focus solely on seeking deliverance, neglecting the joy that comes from living in harmony with God's commandments?

The psalmist's plea for life through God's Word is further emphasized in verse 175: "Let my soul live, and it shall praise thee; and let thy judgments help me." This verse highlights the psalmist's desire for life, both physical and spiritual, with the purpose of offering continuous praise to God. The phrase "let my soul live, and it shall praise thee" indicates that the psalmist sees his life as an opportunity to glorify God, suggesting that the preservation of his life is directly tied to his commitment to worship. The request "let thy judgments help me" reflects the psalmist's reliance on God's righteous decisions to guide and sustain him, recognizing that true help comes from living in accordance with God's judgments. This verse challenges us to consider how we view the purpose of our own lives. Do we, like the psalmist, seek life with the intention of using it to praise and glorify God, relying on His judgments to help us navigate life's challenges, or do we sometimes seek life and help for more self-centered reasons, forgetting the higher purpose of living for God's glory?

The passage concludes in verse 176 with a poignant acknowledgment of the psalmist's need for God's guidance, likening himself to a lost sheep: "I have gone astray like a lost sheep; seek thy servant; for I do not forget thy commandments." This final verse reveals the psalmist's humility and awareness of his own spiritual vulnerability, recognizing that he has "gone astray" and is in need of God's guidance and rescue. The metaphor of the lost sheep suggests a sense of helplessness and dependence, highlighting the psalmist's recognition that he cannot find his way back on his own. The plea "seek thy servant" reflects the psalmist's trust in God's willingness to pursue and bring him back, underscoring the idea that God is the Good Shepherd who cares for His flock. Despite his acknowledgment of having gone astray, the psalmist reaffirms his commitment to God's Word with the statement "for I do not forget thy commandments," indicating that even in his moments of weakness and wandering, he remains devoted to God's teachings. This verse challenges us to reflect on our own spiritual journeys. Do we, like the psalmist, acknowledge our moments of wandering and our need for God's guidance, trusting that He will seek and restore us, and do we remain committed to His commandments even when we feel lost, or do we sometimes allow our spiritual failures to distance us from God, forgetting that He is always ready to guide us back to the path of righteousness?

As we explore the theme of doxology in Psalm 119, verses 169-176, we are reminded of the importance of offering praise, seeking understanding, and reaffirming our commitment to God's Word, even as we acknowledge our need for His guidance and mercy. The psalmist's example challenges us to consider how we approach our relationship with God's Word, particularly in terms of our dedication to praise, our desire for understanding, and our dependence on God's guidance. Do we, like the psalmist, cry out to God with a sincere desire for understanding and deliverance, offering continuous praise as we learn from His Word and trusting in His righteous judgments to guide and sustain us? Do we acknowledge our moments of spiritual wandering and our need for God's guidance, trusting that He will seek us out and restore us to the path of righteousness, even as we remain committed to His commandments?

Furthermore, the psalmist's deep love for God's precepts, his disciplined practice of praise, and his recognition of the peace and joy that come from living according to God's law challenge us to deepen our own commitment to living according to Scripture. Are we willing to make praise and worship a regular and intentional part of our daily lives, acknowledging God's righteousness and justice in all circumstances? Do we recognize that true peace, joy, and understanding are found in loving God's law and living in accordance with His Word, and do we strive to keep His precepts with our whole soul, loving them exceedingly and allowing them to guide every aspect of our lives?

In conclusion, the theme of doxology in Psalm 119, verses 169-176, offers a powerful reminder of the need to anchor our lives in the praise, understanding, and guidance that come from a deep and unwavering commitment to God's Word. The psalmist's unwavering trust in God's mercy and righteousness, his deep commitment to praising God's righteous judgments, and his acknowledgment of his need for God's guidance challenge us to deepen our own devotion to Scripture. As we continue to explore the depths of Psalm 119, may we be inspired to reaffirm our commitment to God's Word, seeking the strength, guidance, and peace that come from a life fully devoted to His commandments, and recognizing that it is through our love for and obedience to Scripture that we find the true purpose, guidance, and fulfillment we need to navigate the complexities and challenges of life.

Whether we are seeking to grow in our understanding of God's Word, striving to live a life that honors God, or facing moments of spiritual wandering and uncertainty, may we always turn to His Word as our source of strength, guidance, and inspiration, knowing that it is through our love for His commandments that we find the true peace, deliverance, and purpose we need to live a life that is fully devoted to Him. The psalmist's example reminds us that true doxology—true praise and worship—is not found in empty words or rituals, but in a life that is fully anchored in the truth and guidance of God's Word. By placing our trust in God's Word and seeking His guidance in every aspect of our lives, we can experience the peace, strength, and fulfillment that come from living a life that is anchored in the truth of

His commandments. As we continue to journey through Psalm 119, may we be encouraged to deepen our commitment to seeking doxology—praise, understanding, and guidance—through God's Word, finding in it the strength, guidance, and inspiration we need to live a life that is fully devoted to Him, anchored in the truth of God's eternal Word.

Conclusion

As we reach the conclusion of "Anchored in Truth: Exploring the Depths of Psalm 119," we are reminded that this journey through Scripture has been more than just an exploration of ancient words; it has been a call to action, a challenge to anchor our lives in the eternal truth of God's Word. Psalm 119 is a profound testament to the power of Scripture, demonstrating how the Word of God is not only a guide but the very foundation of a life lived in faith. Through each verse, the psalmist has shown us the depth of commitment, the strength of conviction, and the peace that comes from aligning every aspect of our lives with God's commandments.

The challenge before us now is to take what we have learned and apply it to our daily walk with God. Psalm 119 is a blueprint for living a life that is fully anchored in truth, where the Word of God is not merely read but cherished, where His commandments are not just obeyed but loved. It calls us to a deeper level of devotion, where our hearts are set on seeking God with our whole being, and our minds are constantly renewed by the wisdom found in His statutes. This psalm is a reminder that true faith is not passive; it requires active engagement with God's Word, a relentless pursuit of understanding, and a steadfast commitment to live out His teachings.

As we reflect on the themes of Psalm 119—such as dedication, delight, dependence, and devotion—we are called to examine our own lives. Are we truly living in a way that reflects the psalmist's passion for God's Word? Do we seek God's guidance in every decision, find joy in His commandments, and trust in His promises even in the face of trials? The psalmist's journey is one of constant growth and transformation, and it invites us to embark on a similar path, where our lives are continually shaped and refined by the truth of Scripture.

But this journey is not without its challenges. The world around us often pulls us in directions that are contrary to God's Word, tempting us to compromise our faith or to neglect our spiritual growth. Psalm 119 serves as a powerful reminder that we must remain vigilant, that we must hold fast to the truth even when it is difficult, and that we must continually seek God's help to stay on the path of righteousness. The psalmist's cry for understanding, his pleas for deliverance, and his declarations of love for God's law are all expressions of a faith that is deeply anchored in the truth, and they challenge us to cultivate the same unwavering commitment.

As you close this book, I encourage you to take the lessons of Psalm 119 to heart and to make them a living reality in your own life. Let the Word of God be your anchor in every storm, your guide in every decision, and your source of joy in every circumstance. May you be inspired to live with the same passion, dedication, and love for God's Word that the psalmist so beautifully exemplifies. And as you continue to explore the depths of Scripture, may your life be richly blessed and transformed by the truth that endures forever.

Don't miss out!

Visit the website below and you can sign up to receive emails whenever Joshua Rhoades publishes a new book. There's no charge and no obligation.

https://books2read.com/r/B-A-AJLBB-VFEYE

BOOKS 2 READ

Connecting independent readers to independent writers.

Did you love *Anchored In Truth Exploring The Depths of Psalm 119*?
Then you should read *Courage Under Fire: David's Stand On The
Battlefield*[1] by Joshua Rhoades!

Courage Under Fire: David's Stand on the Battlefield" recounts the
stirring first-person narrative of David, a young shepherd boy who
faced the colossal Philistine warrior, Goliath, armed with nothing but a
sling, a few stones, and an unwavering faith in God. My journey begins
with my humble obedience to my father, Jesse, who sent me to deliver
provisions to my brothers on the front lines. Despite their scoffing and
jeers at my presence on the battlefield, I remained undeterred, feeling a
deep sense of duty not only to my family but also to the cause they were
fighting for. This sense of duty brought me before King Saul, who, upon
hearing my bold offer to fight Goliath, expressed severe doubts about

1. https://books2read.com/u/3G7wPP

2. https://books2read.com/u/3G7wPP

my abilities. He looked upon my youthful frame and could not see how I, with no armor or sword, could face such a fearsome giant.Goliath himself, towering and menacing, mocked me as I stepped onto the battlefield, his words heavy with contempt and surety of victory. His towering figure clad in armor, with a spear like a weaver's beam, seemed invincible. Yet, as he taunted me, I felt a profound calm settle over me; I knew that the battle was not mine but the Lord's. I declared as much to Goliath, telling him that the God of the armies of Israel whom he had defied would deliver him into my hands. With a simple sling and a stone, and faith as my greatest weapon, I struck the Philistine on his forehead. The giant fell face down to the ground, and I stood over him, a boy no longer underestimated but recognized as the instrument through which God showed His power.This historical moment is not merely a testament to my personal courage but serves as a beacon of inspiration for every Christian facing their own "Goliaths." Whether these giants are doubts, fears, or seemingly insurmountable challenges, the story exemplifies how faith in God equips us to overcome them. The practical lessons derived from this experience emphasize the importance of obedience, humility, and trust in God's power over our own. In moments of trial, we, like I once did, can draw strength from understanding that God's purposes will prevail over our adversities. As I recount my stand on the battlefield, it becomes clear that true victory in life comes from putting our faith into action, trusting in the Lord's guidance, and stepping forward with courage, even when the odds seem overwhelmingly against us.